PREFACE

These few pages contain the outlines of the Administration of Justice of Muslim Law. I have treated it as an historical narrative. I have surveyed the progress of the Muslim Law, during the era of the Holy Prophet, Al-Khulafa-ur-rashidun, the Umayyad, the Abbaside and the Fatimid Khilafat in Spain, in the Turkish Empire and Egypt, in Persia, and finally in India during the reigns of the early Muslim monarchs, the Mughal Emperors and the East India Company practically till the events of 1862. I hope the work will meet with the approval of those interested in the Muslim Jurisprudence.

MAHOMED ULLAH

Law Department,
University of Allahabad.

PUBLISHER'S NOTE

This brochure outlines the main features of the Islamic System of Administration of Justice. Exhaustive yet concise, the treatment accorded is that of a historical narrative so that far from being boring it affords a very pleasant and interesting reading. It traces the development of the law beginning from the era of the Holy Prophet (peace be upon him) continuing through the periods of Khulafa-i-Rashidin, the Umayyads, the Abbaside and the Fatimid Caliphate, the Muslim suzerainty over parts of Europe and Spain, the Turkish Empire and the Muslim rule in Egypt, Persia, and India and ending with the fall of the Mughal Empire.

Crammed with information, beautifully printed, objective in tone and written in a graceful style this brochure is a real contribution to legal history and is a fine example of what such histories should be. It is hoped that Legislators and research scholars of law would derive much benefit from this work of great authority.

CONTENTS

CONTENTS

INTRODUCTION

BY

Mr. Justice Hamoodur Rehman
Formerly Chief Justice of Pakistan

The administration of Justice has always been regarded as one of the great ends of every civilized Government. But the importance given to it by Islam may well be gathered from the fact that "Justice" is considered to be an attribute of God and the Administration of Justice as the performance of a religious duty. The ideal of justice set-up by the Holy Qur'an is the "Mizan" or "balance of justice" and justice has been placed next to piety.

The Holy Qur'an ordains in Sura 55, verses 7-9 :—

> "He has set up the balance (of justice). In order that ye may not transgress (due) balance. So establish weight with justice and fall not short in the balance."

Again in Sura 5, verse 9 Allah ordains :—

> "O' ye who believe ! Stand out firmly for God, as witnesses to fair dealing, and let not the hatred of others to you make you swerve to wrong and depart from Justice. Be just : that is Next to Piety : and fear God, for God is well-acquainted with all that ye do."

The above clearly indicates that the justice or "Adal" according to Islamic concepts demands a perfect standard of comparison, estimation or judgment. It is much more than the distributive or remedial justice of the Greeks, the formal justice of the Romans or even the natural justice of the Anglo-American common law. Its fountain head is the Holy Book.

The Administration of justice consists of the application of the sacred principles of the Shariah in the name of God without any temporal consideration. The dispensation of "Adal" or justice is the exercise of "Al'qada", which according to Islamic concepts is the common concern of all Muslims as a "Furd-al-Kifaya" yet it is requisite that person who administers justice must possess certain basic qualifications. He must be a man of understanding, upright, trustworthy, patient and firm. He must also possess the qualifications necessary for a witness, *i.e.* he must be a free man, adult, sane, Muslim and one who has not been convicted for false accusation (L'ian). There is lack of unanimity on the question as to whether he should also be learned in the 'fiqah' and procedure. As a matter of practice, however, such great care was taken that only very learned and religious scholars should be selected for this high office that later this became the rule (*vide* Mejelle, Minhaj and Hedaya).

The next fundamental principle of Islam is that sovereignty over the universe vests in God. Two important consequences flow from this. The first is that justice has to be administered not only in his name but also according to his teachings, and the second is that every one is equal before the law. No one howhighsoever is immune from the law Allah says in Sura 5 : verse 51 :—

"Surely We have revealed the Book to you with the Truth so that you may judge by means of that which Allah hath taught you."

Again in Sura 4 : Verse 135 Allah ordains :—

'O'ye who believe ; Stand out firmly for justice, as witnesses To God, even as against Yourselves, or your parents, or your kin, and whether It be (against) rich or poor : For God can best protect both. Follow not the lusts (of your hearts), lest ye Swerve, and if ye Distort (Justice) or decline To do justice, verily God is well-acquainted with all that ye do."

During his lifetime the Holy Prophet (p. b. o. h.) administered justice according to the Holy Book, but since his interpretation of the Qur'anic Ayats was naturally expected to be the most accurate and his personality also reflected the Holy Qur'an in its letter and spirit, his decisions became precedents for the future and what he decided became "Ahadith" and ranked as the next most important source of Shariah law. He was famous for his impartiality. Even non-Muslims brought their disputes to him. He always, according to Divine dictates, treated everyone as equal before the law including himself and gave equal protection to all yet he never claimed infallability. Very often when he himself was in doubt he received revelations giving him the solution of his doubts. He did not hesitate to point out, however, that he decided the cases before him upon the evidence adduced and that he was liable to err in forming his judgment like other human beings. The revelation of the shares of female heirs in Sura Nissa, it is reported according to Jabir, was made when a waman brought her two daughters before the Holy Prophet and complained that their uncle had taken away all the property left by her deceased husband and that it was not possible for her to get her daughters married without property. This was the rule according to the customary law of ancient Arabia. The Holy Prophet desisted from giving any answer saying that God alone could decide this point. Thereafter the verse was revealed. The Holy Prophet thereafter sent for the woman and the uncle and told him to give 2/3 to the two daughters and 1/8 to the widow and to take all that remained after such distribution. Similarly the Qur'anic Sura XXIV was revealed when the Holy Prophet was deciding the case of accusation of adultery by Hilal Bin Ummayyah against his wife (Sura XXIV : Verses 4-10).

The Holy Prophet not only did not consider himself to be above the law but also sought to establish this by his own acts and precepts. He established the important constitutional principle that the Head of any Islamic State could be sued both as a private individual and also in respect of his public acts. During his Last Sermon at the Hajjatul Wada the Holy Prophet, in fact, testified to his love for justice and equality by publicly declaring to community that if he owed anything to anyone or had misappropriated anyone's property or had done any harm to anyone's life or reputation he was present there to pay his dues to whomsoever demanded it. The audience was amazed and out of the whole assembly there was only one person who claimed some Dirhams which were paid promptly.

Jabir also, according to the Al-Hadit compiled by Muslim, reported that the Messenger of Allah said :—

> "As for what follows next the best guidance is the guidance of Muhammad (p. b. o. h.). The worst of forces is their innovation and every innovation is misleading."

Even during his lifetime the Holy Prophet him self, after the spread of Islam throughout Arabia, appointed functionaries for different parts of the Peninsula. At first the Provincial Governors were invested also with judicial powers but later on the practice grew up of appointing a judge (Cadi) in addition. In Medina itself the judicial power was not delegated to any other functionary but to the Savants of Medina who had embraced the religion. In other provinces however, an independent functionary was deputed to administer justice.

The Holy Prophet had in his lifetime also introduced the Department of "Al-Mazalim" which had a special jurisdiction of compelling persons doing each other wrong (Mutazalimun), to do mutual justice and restraining litigants from refuting claims by inspiring fear and awe in them. This was a wide and general jurisdiction both correctional and remedial in nature. It is reported that in the exercise of this jurisdiction the Holy Prophet himself decided a case of a dispute relating to the priority of right of irrigation.

During the period of the Holy Prophet the procedure was naturally simple but the presence of the parties was necessary to the settlement of a dispute. Even at this early stage the rule had been laid down that the burden of proof lay upon the asserting party and the defendant had to deny on oath the plaintiff's claim. Upon such denial the plaintiff was to prove his case but if the defendant refused to take the oath the case could be decreed

Possession was also regarded as *prima facie* proof of the right to hold the property. Thus if evidence of both sides claiming the property was equal the decision would go in favour of the person in possession. The evidence of an adulterer, a person noted for dishonesty, or of a slave in favour of his master was, however, not admissible.

According to another Hadith reported in Abu Dawood and also in Tirmizy, the Holy Prophet also permitted the use of Qiyas in deciding cases. It is reported that when the Apostle of God sent Mu'az bin Jabal to Yemen he asked him as to how he would decide cases brought before him. Mu'az replied:—

"I will judge by the Qur'an"

The Prophet said, "If you do not find any solution in the Book of God."

Mu'az replied, "then I will decide in accordance with the Traditions of the Holy Prophet."

The Prophet said, "and if thou do not find anything in the Traditions."

Mu'az replied, "then I will decide according to my own judgment and will not slacken effort."

Thereupon the Prophet said: "Praise be to God Who has caused the Messenger of the Apostle of God to agree with what the Apostle of God likes."

After the Holy Prophet, the Khulafa-e-Rashidin also followed the same lofty principles of administration of justice, During the Khilafat of Hazrat Abu Bakr, Hazrat Umar was appointed the Qazi but the people were so contended and honest that according to the author of Seerat-us-Siddique (M. Habib-ur-Rahman Khan) not a single case was filed in the Court of Umar. In this period, however, the use of the Ijma' and Ijtihad were introduced.

The Second Khalifa Hazrat Umar bin Al-Khattab separated the judicial office. It was clearly made independent from the other offices of the State. He appointed Abu Dardah as Judge within Medina, Abu Musa Al-Ashari as Judge in Kufa and Qazi Shurayah as Judge in Basra. This separation marks the beginning of an important era in the history of administration of justice in the Muslim world. It is this which led Von Hammar (*vide* Ameer Ali History of Saracens, p. 62) to say :

> "The Judge was named and is still named the "Hakim-ush-Shara'a, *i. e.*, ruler through the law, for law rules through the utterance of justice, and power of the Governor carries out the utterance of it. Thus the Islamite Administration, even in its infancy, proclaims in word and in deed the necessary separation between judicial and executive power."

In the famous Firman sent by Hazart Umar to Abu Musa Ashari the Qazi's functions are laid down as follows :—

> "After the praise to God the administration of Justice is a duty. The Court must observe equality between the parties so that the weaker party may expect justice and the stronger may not expect concession. The burden of proof is on the plaintiff and the defendant may be put on oath, but let this not defeat the ends of justice and law. If you have decided a case, then after due care and thinking you may revise your decision. If you are doubtful in a point which is mentioned in the Kor'an and Hadis then think over it again and again and then apply "Qiyas" (a process of deduction). When a party wants to tender evidence then fix a time limit and if he proves his case then decide accordngly. All Muslims are fit to be witnesses except those who have received the prescribed punishment (flogging) for *hadd* (fornication, adultery) and those who have tendered false evidence."

The Firman sent to Kazi Shurayah, in the words of the Kazi himself, was as follows :—

> "It is related by Shurayah that Umar wrote to him, that if a case is presented to him which is treated in the Kor'an then decide accordingly and do not go against the Kor'anic Injunctions, and if such a case is presented to him which

is not treated in the Kor'an, then follow it in the Hadith and decide accordingly, but if a case is presented to him about which there is no provision in the Kor'an and Hadith, then look for its solution in the Ijma-ul-Umat and follow that decision. However if such a case is presented to you about which there is no precedent in the Kor'an and Hadith, and not even decided by anyone before you then you may decide it according to your own judgment after due care and caution. I approve of such course."

According to there Firmans it is clear that under the Islamic system of administration of justice the burden of proof lies on the plaintiff and that the judge can rely on his private judgment (Qiyas) provided the judgment is not against the provisions of Qur'an and Sunnah and the Judge may review his own judgment.

Hazart Umar like his predecessors also decided points on which no directive was given in the Holy Qur'an or no precedent of the Holy Prophet was available by Ijma by debating on the point in the assembly of the Ashab of the Holy Prophet. He also often resorted to Ijtihad. He granted an irrevocably divorced woman maintenance although a Hadith to the contrary was cited before him. He preferred to rely upon the Qur'anic Injunction which gave a divorced woman the right of residence on the ground that the person who reported the Hadith did not remember it correctly. The Shafe'is, however, follow the Hadith and they allow no maintenance to such a woman unless she be pregnant.

In another case Hazrat Umar created a new precedent by accepting the evidence of an expert in a defamatory suit filed by Zibriqan bin Badr against a poet Hutaya. The verse in dispute was not clear Hence he summoned another poet Hassan bin Sabit and decided the case according to the latter's opinion.

He also like the Holy Prophet submitted to the Supremacy of the law. In a suit brought against a Jew by Hazrat Umar, both went to the Qazi. The latter on seeing the Khalifa rose in his seat out of deference Hazrat Umar considered this such an unpardonable weakness that he dismissed the Qazi at once. On another occasion when Hazrat Umar found his own son Abu Shama drunk he had him publicly flogged. He also started the practice of giving suitable allowances to the persons who held the posts of Qazis so that they should not be in want. But he also prohibited them from taking part in any business.

Umar did not create separate criminal Courts. The same courts had jurisdiction over both civil and criminal matters. However, in criminal matters the proceedings were initiated by the Department of Police, technically known as "Ahdas". The Officer-in-Charge of this Department was known as "Sahibul Ahdas"

He was also the first to set up Jails by setting apart a building in Mecca as a public jail. Thereafter jails were built in other places also. The introduction of the jail system resulted in the substitution of many of the harsh punishments provided in Islam by confinement in jails. He also introduced the sentence of transportation and also suspended the Hadd punishment for theft during a period of acute scarcity of food. Hazrat Umar also clarified that cases were to be decided not merely on the basis of the number of witnesses but on the basis of truth as the essential principle of the Qur'anic teaching was that justice could only be done on the basis of unimpeachable evidence.

The origin of the Muslim law of Waqfs is also traced to a dedication made by Hazrat Umar. It is related in the Tirmizy that Hazrat Umar sought the Holy Prophet's advice to make pious use of a piece of land he had acquired in Khaiber. The Holy Prophet advised him, it is reported, in the following terms:—

> "Tie up the property (asl., corpus) and devote the usufruct to human beings, and it is not to be sold or made the subject of gift or inheritance; devote its produce to your children, your kindred and the poor in the way of God."

No special changes took place in the time of 3rd Khalifa, Usman, Hazrat Ali (the 4th Khalifa), who was a great jurist and the most learned lawyer of his time, followed the practice of his predecessors and upheld the use of Ijma as also resorted to Ijtihad. He is regarded as the founder of the doctrine of increase, Awl in the law of inheritance. He too upheld the supremacy of the law. In a suit for the recovery of his armour from a Jew in the court of the Qazi of Kufa he appeared personally but lost the case because the only witnesses he had in support of his claim were his slave and his son. None of these were competent witnesses under Islamic Law. Judgment was given in favour of the Jew. But the Jew was so highly moved by the justice of Islam that he embraced Islam and gave the armour back to Hazrat Ali.

With the assasination of Hazrat Ali, however, the republican period of Islam ended. But the firm foundation on which the system had been placed by the Khulafa-i-Rashideen survived. The system of Judicial administration remained more or less the same even under the Umayyads. However, special care was taken in appointing to the office only persons who owned loyalty to the executive head and belonged either to the same family or shared in status as clients. The Qazis were appointed and dismissed publicly. There were Qazis with limited jurisdiction as also unlimited jurisdiction. Those with limited jurisdiction were restricted either to the duties or to the territory specified in the Firman of Appointment but the others had extensive jurisdiction with full powers over all things authorised by law.

The important change that took place in this period is that Judges were burdened with certain other executive duties. Such as the appointment of guardians of infants, the administration of Waqf Properties, execution of punishments prescribed by law, looking after testamentary dispositions, supervision of Subordinate Qazis and other law officers such as notaries and secretaries. There was no regular court of appeal but usually the Sovereign himself performed the duties of a High Court of appeal. In the reign of Khalifa Al-Mamoon a Nazir-il-Muzalim or Board for the Inspection of Grievances was also set up. The Sovereign himself presided over this Board which. included the Chief Qazi, the Chief Wazir and one or two secretaries of State and jurists or Muftis. This Board also controlled the judiciary and could correct miscarriages of justice.

The Ummayyads did not also have separate criminal courts. The Judges were entrusted with both civil and criminal jurisdiction. This gave them wide discretionary powers which they could utilize for restraining litigation. There was no prescribed procedure to be followed in criminal cases. Although evidence was taken, both direct and circumstantial, yet attempts were made to bring about reconciliation between litigants often with success. Since the Khalifa himself sat in this court it could also check cases of injustice by Members of the royal family and high officials. It is through this Muzalim jurisdiction that the judges also came to exercise influence over the Sovereign and to acquire jurisdiction to review executive acts like those exercised under the writ jurisdiction.

We now come to the Abbaside period. It is during this period that the science of jurisprudence flourished and attained its golden age. It is in this age that traditions were collected, commentaries on the Qur'an were written and the sciences of the sources were developed. The four great schools of Sunni Law namely ; Hanafe'i, Shafi, Maliki and Hanbali, became established. The administration of justice was conducted on definite lines which bear close similarities to the modern systems. The Abbasides, like their predecessors, attached extreme importance to the Administration of Justice and the Department of Justice was called "Darul Adal". The Chief Justice of the Empire was called "Qadi-ul-Qaddat". He was the Head of the Darul Adal and was independent from executive control. The subordinate judiciary was placed under him and each city possessed its own Qazi. In big towns, there were also Deputy Qadis or Naib Qadis. Their functions and jurisdiction were generally the same as those of judges under the Umayyad Dynasty. The Abbasides also developed a procedure for consulting specialists in the Shariah Law through Muftis and jurists who also assisted the litigants with written opinions or 'fatwas'. In this way the Department of Justice acquired a permanent relationship with the law and became a more vigorous institution. But Khalifas under the Persian influence retained the right to receive complaints and hear appeals as a final court to set right cases of miscarriage of justice through the Dewan-un-Mazalim or the Board for the Inspection of Grievances. This Board was presided over by the Sovereign himself or in his absence by a Special Officer known as the President, other members of the Board included the Chief Justice, the Hajib *i. e.* Chief Door-keeper, who was responsible for the protection of the Khalifa against the free access of petitioners, the principal Secretaries of State .(Wazirs) and some nominated Muftis or Jurists.

The status of the President of this Board was higher than that of Qadis who were under its supervision and control. The powers of the President were also very wide. He was not bound by the strict letter of the law. He had the power to apply the principles of equity to secure the ends of justice. The Board not only could supervise and correct miscarriages of justice by Qazi but could also correct the cases of injustice and tyranny committed against the people by the Governors of the Provinces. Injustices in the levy of taxes, claims for illegal reduction or withholding of pay of Government servants, claims for the restoration of property taken by force, the governance of Auqaf and the suppression of open evil cases which were not suppressed due to the weakness of the Muhtasibs also came within the jurisdiction of this Board.

The Muhtaṣib or Public Censor was responsible for the enforcement of moral duties and obligations. This was in accordance with the Qur'anic Injunctions. The power of the Muhtasib also exceeded the power of the Qazi for the reason that he could act *suo motu* and was invested with powers to enforce obedience to the commandments of Allah by striking fear. His duties were concerned with matters relating to :—

(1) Whatever was due to God ;
(2) Whatever was due to men : and
(3) To both.

Under the first head came such matters as the enforcement on the community the duty of observance of p ayers, fastings and other religious acts. The second covered all matters relating to the public, individually and collectively, such as non-payment of debts without excuse and even failure of water supply. The third concerned such matters as irrigation rights, rights of way, easements or nuisances. The Muhtasib's jurisdiction was indeed very wide. He could even draw the attention of the Qadi to the delay, if any, in the disposal of cases or inconveniences, if any, being caused to the litigants. The Muhtasib also exercised disciplinary control over Attorneys and Vakils. They saw to it that Vakils were not bought over by the other party or encouraged tampering with the administration of justice.

The Administration of Criminal Justice in this period became separated and was placed in the hands of Magistrates who were called "Sahibul Mazalim". This jurisdiction could also be exercised by Wazirs and Governors with full powers but if their powers were limited then they had to obtain special mandates from the Khalifa. Such Magistrates supplemented the authority of the Qadis and also were responsible for securing compliances with the decrees of the Qadis more or less as Courts of execution.

The system of Court officials which had developed by the third century of the Hijra was that under the Qadi there was a *katib* who kept the record of the cases. He combined in him the functions of the registrar and the Court clerk. The *muzakki* investigated the character of the ordinary witnesses, the *murtarjim* translated their statements. The Awans or auxiliaries maintained order within the Court. In addition to them there was a Doorkeeper, "*bawwab*", who assisted it in the maintenance of order. The *Ammal-ul-Hakam* looked after the properties of orphans under the supervision of the Qadi and the *Khazin Diwanul Hakam* maintained the Court archives.

The procedure followed in civil matters was as already indicated earlier that the Judge treated the parties appearing before h m in an impartial manner.

All litigants, no matter how high or how low, were treated as equals. He listened to their respective pleadings without giving any sign of approbation or blame. First called upon the plaintiff to address. This was followed by the defendant's address. Where the claim of plaintiff was also denied on oath, the plaintiff was called upon to produce evidence. Witnesses produced before the Courts for giving evidence had to be competent witnesses and persons of proved honesty. The persons who had been convicted for robbery or of drunkenness or adultery or false accusation or had the reputation of being persons of bad moral character were not allowed to give evidence. These matters were determined on the basis of the report of the *muzzaki*.

At one stage this led to the practice of having a prepared list of competent witnesses but this was forbidden by law as the Qazis had no right to designate any one in advance of being competent to depose before him. If the case was settled or terminated by a decision, a judgment had to follow and this was incorporated in a decree or *hukum*. The Judge had also the right to pass an *ex parte* decree but only if the defendant was residing at a considerable distance. The Judge had also the power to review his own judgment if it was later found to be against the Qur'an or Sunnah.

Parties to a litigation could also appear through representatives appointed in accordance with the Islamic law of Agency or Mandate, called a *vakil*. The latter submitted his power of attorney or *tawakkil* to the Qadi before being allowed to plead. The origin of this practice lay in the unique place acquired by the Ulema and Muftis in this period by their official association in the administration of justice as advisers to Governors and Qadis. It was only a further extension of this advice to litigants as well at their request ; originally gratis but later on a fee. This practice became so well-recognized in Muslim states that it came to be recognized as a responsibility of the State to provide citizens with such *legal aid* and the Muftis became the first legal practitioners in the Islamic system and as under the present system, they became a necessary adjunct to the administration of justice.

The law also made it obligatory that for the protection of the interests of minors, insane persons or those suffering from legal incompetence a competent representative should be present. If the person did not have such a competent person it became the duty of the Court to appoint one for him.

Joinder of parties was also permissible if necessary for doing complete justice.

On the criminal side the complainant was required to give a precise account of the offence mentioning whether it was premeditated or voluntary or whether there was any accomplice or not. If he failed to do that, the Court could dismiss the complaint on the ground that no *prima facie* case had been made out.

Apart from this there was no specified rule of procedure. But fair trial was considered necessary. It is reported that a woman once complained before the Court presided over by Khalifa Almamoon that a State official had forcibly dispossessed her from her lands which she had inherited from her husband and son. The Khalifa directed her to appear on a fixed date. When she appeared and was asked as to who that official was, she replied that it was the Khalifa's son, named; Abbas, who was standing next to him. The Khalifa ordered the Qazi to make the accused sit with the woman and then take down their respective statements. Her lands were *ad interim* ordered to be restored to her. But the case was directed to be heard by a Deputy because of the rule which disqualified a person from adjudicating in his own son's case.

This shows you that the principles of equality, fairness and natural justice ; that a person should not be a Judge in his own cause or be liable to be biased were all known to the Islamic system of jurisprudence and only observed long before they came to be recognized in the West.

Later developments under Ottomans of Turkey and the muslim rulers of India mainly affected the constitutional position of the sovereign who began to style himself as Zille Allah or Shadow of God on earth and to claim the right to legislate by his edicts. This did not, however, mean that imperial edicts could override the Qur'an and Sunnah of the Prophet. The edicts came in the shape of Qanun-Namahs in regard to ecclesiastical or temporal problems not provided for by the Shariah. Codifications were made from time to time in Turkey starting from 1545 C. E. when a code called Sultan Sulaiman's Qanun-Namah came into existence. This was followed by the Hatti Sherif, the Commercial Code, the Penal Code, the Civil Procedure Code and the Book of Rules of Justice popularly known as the Mejelle. The latter codified the Islamic principles relating to sale, hire, guarantee, debts, pledges, trusts, agency, joint ownership, admissions, actions evidence and administration of justice.

In the Ottoman judicial set up the Skeikh-ul-Islam and two Qadi-Askers of Rumelia and Anatolia came at the top. Below them were the Great Mullahs in the capital and the main cities. Then came senior and junior Mullah and the lowest cadre consisted of ordinary Qadis and their Naibs. As under the Abbasides there were also Muftis with the Grand Mufti and Sheikh-ul-Islam at the top. The Muftis alone could issue fatwas and also give legal assistance and guidance to the Qadis, Governors and lay litigants. They were organised into an official aministrative hierarchy. They were appointed for life and they often exercised effective constitutional check upon the sovereign's prerogative and restrained the passing of arbitrary laws.

The structure of the Courts was similar to those under Abbasides but there were also secular Courts set up under the provisions of various Codes. These were called the Nizamiah. In addition there were Diwan Courts to try capital cases against high officials and the sentences passed by the latter were executed by an official known as the "Chaush". Death sentences had to be confirmed by the Sovereign who acted as the ultimate Court of appeal.

It may be mentioned here that the Turkish Penal Code of 1858 did not approve of the Hadd penalty for theft and the Civil Procedure Code of 1880 permitted a legal rate of interest in case of ordinary commercial loans.

Under the Muslim rulers of India also the institutions of Government were similar to those adopted by the abbasides although the nomenclature of the officials varied from time to time. The Shariat law formed the basis of judicial administration supplemented by "Firman". Even under Aurangzeb's reign the Emperor was "the ocean of justice". His Court, which consisted of the Emperor, the Qadis, Muftis and Adils, was the highest Court of appeal. Civil and Criminal justice was administered through the Qadi-ul-Qaddat who in turn appointed local Qadis. The Sadr-us-Sudur or Sadr-i-Jehan was the Chief Civil Judge.

The functions of Judges were regulated by the "Adab" or literature of the Shariah which had by now become formalised but more or less were the same as those under the Abbasides. These were also codified in the Fatawa-i-Alamgiri which was another condification of Islamic Law and procedure prepared under Aurangzeb s directions. This compilation was so comprehensive that it covered almost every aspect of a Muslim's individual and social life according to the Hanafi School. It became and still is the most authoritative book of reference of Shariah law and Islamic judicial institutions. Even in this regime which sought to enforce Islamic laws and Islamic penalties strictly specific directions were issued regarding the imposition of Hadd penalties. Thus into the Diwan of Gujrat in 1672 a 'firman' was directed to the following effect :—

> "When theft is rife in the town and a thief is captured, do not even after proof behead him nor impale him as it may be his first offence. If a man has committed theft only once either less than or only up to the amount or Nisab... then chastise (ta'zir) him. But if he repeats the offence, then after ta'zir keep him in prison till he repents. If he is not cured by ta'zir and imprisonment, but commits theft again, then sentence him to long-term imprisonment, or Siyasat and execution, and restore the stolen property to the owner, after legal proof of ownership if he is present. Otherwise deposit the property in trust (amanah) in the Bait al-Mal."

The Moghal Emperors also maintained the institution of Muftis and allowed legal representation of litigants.

With the change in the concept of sovereignty, however, the strict theory of Islamic jurisprudence that no one was above the law underwent some modification. The Khalifa or Sultan was given immunity from punishment in respect of certain crimes. The Hedaya states the rule in very cautious terms, as follows :—

> "If a Supreme ruler (such as the Khalifa for the time being) commit any offence punishable by Law, such as whoredom, theft or drunkenness, he is not subject to any punishment (but yet if he commit murder he is subject to the Law of retaliation and he is also accountable in matters of property)—because punishment is a right of God, the infliction of which is committed to the Khalifa (or other Supreme Magistrate) and to none else, and he cannot inflict punishment upon himself as in this there is no advantage, because the good proposed in punishment is that it may operate as a warning to deter mankind from sin, and this is not obtained by a person inflicting punishment upon himself, contrary to the rights of the individual such as the laws of retaliation and of propety, the penalties of which may be exacted of the Khalifa as the claimant of right may obtain satisfaction either by the Khalifa empowering him to exact his right from himself, or by the claimant appealing for assistance to the collective body of the Mussulmans."

The tendency to avoid infliction of the Hadd punishment, as far as possible, grew with time and both in the Ottoman and Moghul empires the punishment for Sarika was modified. The Turkish Penal Code ultimately abolished the punishment of cutting off of the hand and the Firman sent to the Diwan of Gujrat in 1972 (already quoted indicates the extent of the change effected in the Moghul period.

From the above account of the systems of administration of justice prevailing in Muslim countries under different regimes it can be gathered that the fundamental principles remained, except for minor modifications, unchanged. These were that the Islamic or Shariah Courts from the earliest of times administered justice in public gaze following the adversary system after hearing both parties and considering their evidence. Courts could be held in Mosques, as they were in the beginning, or in other premises to which the public had access until Court buildings, called Dar-ul-Qada were built. Sovereigns, of course, held Court in their Diwans.

Judges were generally selected with care from amongst scholars of repute possessing high moral standards and had to observe a very strict code of conduct. They had to abstain from all actions and deeds which might destroy the "majesty of the Court" (Mejelle). They could not accept presents from litigants or attend a feast given by either party or even meet only one of the parties either at their residence or in their retiring room or speak to one of the parties either by a sign or language unknown to the other. In fact he was required to abstain from any partionaction or circumstance which might cause suspicion of ship or bias. He could not be a Judge in his own cause or in the cause of his near relatives.

The rule of *audi alteram partem* was known to them and they also observed the rules of natural justice and had to record formal judgment and decree so that the same cause may not be tried over again. A previous decree became conclusive and could be tendered in evidence in another Court. The rule of *res judicata* was thus also followed.

Arbitration was permitted but either party could retract before the award. An award when made became conclusive and could be referred to a Qadi. If he agreed with the award he put it into execution in the same manner as a decree. The arbitrator had to possess the same qualifications as a Qadi and was bound by the same code of conduct.

So far as evidence is concerned it could be oral or documentary, direct or circumstantial (Qarinat). Oral testimony could also be direct or hearsay. The latter was only admissible to prove paternity, death and of reliable character. The oral evidence had to come from competent witnesses. The evidence of a slave or one committed for slander or robbery or drunkenness or whoredom or adultery was not admissible nor the evidence in favour of a son, grandson, father, grandfather, husband or wife and *vice versa*. According to the Hanafi School the testimony of atrocious criminals, immodest persons, usurpers, drunkards, falcoaers, public mourners and singers was also inadmissible.

In civil matters a single or isolated testimony called 'Ahad' couid be sufficient but in criminal matters proof had to be furnished by at least two witnesses except in the case of Zina where four witnesses were necessary. In cases liable to be punished by the imposition of the Hadd strict compliance was required with the requirements of legal proof.

The testimony of women was not admissible in cases of punishment and retaliation but in all other cases their evidence was admissible but for one man two women had to give evidence. However in cases which did not admit of the possibility of male inspection *e.g.*, virginity and child birth, female evidence was admissible but according to Imam Shafe'i there had to be at least four female witnesses in such cases.

Judgments could also be passed on the basis of admissions and confessions (Iqrar) and this was indeed quite frequent. The plea in confession and avoidance was also known and the rule of estoppels was quite elaborate (*vide* Mejelle). It could be by statement *e.g.*, admission or release or by conduct *e.g.*, a contradictory claim or by silence provided it was of a conclusive nature (Qatiatun).

There was no period of limitation provided by Shariah but such period could be prescribed by legislation as was done by the Ottoman and Moghuls (*vide* Mejelle and Fatawa-i-Alamgiri). There was also no court-fee in the Islamic system. To administer justice was the duty of the State and it had to be provided free.

Subject to some minor differences you will thus observe the forms trial, at any rate in civil matters, bear such close similarity to the forms of procedure prevalent now that one cannot help enquiring as to from where the present procedures were borrowed. My own theory is that they trickled into Europe through Spain where many European scholars went to study in the famous universities of Cordova, Seville and Granada. The impact of Islam, though not often recognised by European scholars, was so great that it revolutionised their thinking and affected almost every branch of law and legal procedure although in Muslim countries there regrettably descended a period of stagnation.

A HISTORICAL AND COMPARATIVE INTRODUCTION TO THE MUSLIM CONCEPTION OF THE STATE.

The development of the institution of State and the evolution of kingship is a matter of historical interest. It is only true that humanity in its inception had no possible ideal but food and reproduction. Thereafter rudimentary societies grew up. The nomadic tribes were succeeded by villages, and they in turn were replaced by cities and finally by States and Empires. Kingship is a natural evolution of leadership of people in nomadic stages of existence. Biological needs and emotional ambition created civilisations of military types: the mystical forces created civilisations of intense religious nature: the intellectual forces were linked up with the growth of civilizations, but have never asserted themselves independently not even in the modern civilisation. The religious spirit is as intense today as it was in antiquity. The foundation of modern doctrines of the State such as Socialism, Communism, Bolshevism can be traced to antiquity. The world has witnessed the rise and fall of the great States and Empires —The Egyptian the Hellenic, the Roman, the Asiatic monarchies and the Muslim Empires have all passed away. The existence of our modern civilisation is only transient. It is another chapter in the "history of man."

The State is really an association of human beings, established primarily for defence against external enemies and for the maintenance of peace, law and order. According to Jellinek, "Men who command and those who obey their commands make up the substance of the State."[1]. What is the basis for the right to command and duty to obey? "No one has the right to command others, neither an Emperor, nor a king, nor a parliament, nor a popular majority is able to impose its will as such."[2] But the fact remains that the people are ruled by a sovereign power. This power presents itself under different guises, sometimes, it appears as a material force, or as a religious force, and again as an intellectual force and in our present day as an economic force. In all countries and at all times those who are materially, religiously, morally, intellectually, economically, or numerically superior have succeeded in imposing their will upon the subservient.

---

1. Allgemeine Staatslehre p. 169. 2. Duguit, Traite de droit constitutionnel Vol I p. 41.

The idea of a Universal State is inherent in man who is by nature "a political animal." The common nature of mankind implies the need of a Universal State and which idea corresponds to the idea of the universal church."[1]

Universal State.

The Hellenic idea of the State is given by Plato as: "the best State is that which approaches most nearly to the condition of the individual." Aristotle declares the State to be the association of clans and village communities in a complete and self-sufficing life.[3]

Hellenic Idea.[4]

Cicero gives the Roman idea of the State, as the highest product of human virtue (*virtus*) ; as the nearest approach to the will of the Gods[5], and he considered "the State to be the People organised", and that the will of the people was the source of law[6]. The jurist Gaius maintains, " civitas est constitutio populi." The tendency of the Romans was to create a universal Empire. When the power of the Pope was established at Rome the Roman idea of universal dominion was intensified in a spiritual form.

Roman Idea.

The Jewish idea of the State is a divine institution. This is the basis of the Jewish theocracy. In other words God has founded the State, and hence divine government is essential. Christianity also does not conceive the State as outside the divine order.

The Muslim conception of the State is also that of universal dominion, it is akin to theocracy, but the Prophet of Islam did not restore the absolute theocracy of Moses. The Muslim State is an homogenous-religious and political-institution of the Islamic brother-hood. It is a commonwealth of all the Muslims living as one whole under the control and guidance of a supreme executive. In the institution of Khilafat, the ideals of the political system of Islam are combined, the temporal and spiritual functions are vested in the supreme executive. In Islam sovereignty primarily belongs to God, and next to God the sovereign power resides in the people. In Muslim countries "Church and State" are one indissoluble whole, and until the very essence of Islam passes away, that unity cannot be relaxed.[7]

Muslim Idea.

---

1. Bluntschli T. K. The theory of the State p. 25.
2. Rep. V. p. 462. 3. Pol. III 9.
4. In the Hellenic idea too much power was ascribed to the State.
5. Cicero de Rep. 1 7. Neque est ulla res, in qua propius ad Deorum numen virtus accedat humana quam civitates aut condere novas aut conservare jam conditas.
6. The Romans brought out into prominence the legal nature of the State.
7. The author of Akhlak-i-Jalaly (translated by W.F. Thomoson) holds, p. 323 "Life cannot be maintained without society, nor society without government, nor government without religion".

SOVEREIGNTY.

Ancient Community.

The ancient political theory hardly deals with the modern notion of Sovereignty. Plato's republic lays emphasis upon an organisation of the people. Aristotle attempted to formulate the organisation of powers such as monarchy, aristocracy, and democracy. This division does not indicate any distinction between Sovereignty and law. In the Platonic theory as supplimented by Aristotle the central idea is the relation between individual and community, and there is no attempt to formulate precisely a relation between the sovereign and the people. Similarly in the Sotic philosophy the idea of the community as based on natural law is given prominence. In a word the ancient political theory was a theory of the legal order of the community.

Divine Right.

There are two well known theories as regards the origin of government and the obligation of the subject to obey laws made by the Sovereign power. One is the "Patriarchal theory", by which Sovereignty was claimed to be based upon divine right, the other is a social contract theory. For centuries the world has been dominated by the idea of a Sovereign having a subjective right to govern and of subjects conceived as political subordinates. Jein Bodin says "Sovereignty is the Supreme power over citizens and subjects unrestrained by laws[1]." "The Sovereign is the source of law and, as such, cannot be bound by it. He is subject only to the divine law and to the law of nature, and is responsible to God alone for his acts"[2] The ostentatious claim imputed to Louis XIV "I am the State," simply reflects the dominating ideal of that epoch making era.[3] The old German theory was somewhat similar. "The monarch is not an organ of the State, he is the ruler or Sovereign over it." "The royal authority does not rest upon the constitution, the constitution rests upon the royal authority[4]. The Hindu jurists

1. De republica lib I Cap VIII. 2. H. Krabbe, "The Modern idea of the State, p xviii.

3. Bluntschli observes (The Theory of the State p. 288). "The proud words of Louis XIV, We princes are the living images of Him who is all holy and powerful are a blasphemy towards God, and an insult towards his subjects—men as much as he." Just compare this with the remarkable view expressed by T. Morrison, (Imperial rule in India p. 43) referring to the East, there lies upon the eyes and foreheads of all men a law which is not found in the European decalogue and this law runs: 'Thou shalt honour and worship the man whom God shall set above the for thy king: if he cherish thee thou shalt love him; and if he plunders and oppress thee thou shalt still love him, for thou art his slave and his chattel."

4. H. Krabbe The modern idea of the State p. xxv quoting Von Seydel Payerisches staatsrecht.

have also credited the king with the divine right to rule. "The king's office is that of Indra and Yama visible inflictor of punishment, and bestower of reward. On those who despise them even divine punishment descends."[1] Similarly the Sassanian kings of Persia called themselves Gods or divine kings.

When the Muslim republican institutions were trampled down absolute monarchy was established throughout the Muslim world. The Muslim Kings added to the titles of the Khalifa and Imam the renowned appellation of "the shadow of God upon earth"[2] a distiuction undreamt of by the first followers of Islam. This is the nearest approach to the theory of divine right in Islam. The title however was misused. For instance Emperor Akbar the great was regarded as an incarnation of the Supreme Light, and his courtiers misused the Muslim formula "Alahu Akbar," "God is Great" "as meaning Akbar is God.

Middle Ages.

In the middle ages we first find a conception of the State characterized by the opposition between sovereign and subject. When the monarchs had secured their independence against the Church, it was with a view to define the limits of the Sovereign's powers that the theory of Sovereignty received considerable attention. The Greek philosophy again exercised its influence, the idea of community was considered anew, and the theory of the Social contract grew up, which on one hand completely checked the theory of divine right of the Church, and on the other hand limited the authority of the Sovereign. Althusius was the first to formulate that by a contract the community subjected itself to the authority of the Sovereign.

A contrary theory was laid down by Hobbes, to the effect that the community is a product of Sovereign's authority ; that the King receives all his powers from each individual rather than from the community as a whole. He attempted to find a basis for power permanent and inexpugnable; one and indivisible ; absclute and limitless.

---

1. Mr. Jayaswal rejects the theory of divine right andsays (Hindu Polity p. 58) "Divine theory of kingly origin and kingly right could have found soil in Hindu India if there had been no live interest and constitutional jealousy in the people to check such pernicious claims and notions. The Hindu theory of kingship was not permitted to degenerate into a divine imposture and profane autocracy."

2. This title was used by the kings of Persia, India and also by the Ottoman Sultans, see Sir E. Creasy, History of the Ottoman Turks, p. 61.

The Hindu theory of social contract.

The Mahabharata depicts a scene which shows how the ancient Indo-Aryans created a King on the Principle of 'give and take,' 'In days of Yore, when the Earth had no King the people began to devour one another........they had to approach Brahma, the Creator, whom they addressed thus, Lord we are being annihilated for want of a king. Grant us therefore a king. We all will adore him, and he will protect us in return.......Brahma asked Manu to take up the duty of protecting them but Manu declined the honour saying : 'I am always afraid of committing a wrong and sinful act.'.........Then the people addressed themselves to Manu, saying, 'Lord, do not thou be afraid of anything, sin will never touch thee. We will fill up the royal treasury by contributing into it heads of cattle, a fiftieth share of gold, and tenth share of grain........ those who are capable of bearing arms and riding will follow thee, as the Gods follow Indra'.. ....the people thus saying the powerful Manu ...... issued forth from his castle, on a blaze of glory, followed by innumerable armed men, with a view to take up the duty of protecting the people (Santi Parva Ch. 67.)" The above account also establishes the theory that the kings were elected by the people and election depended upon their personal qualifications and during the nomadic age on physical strength. It is said that "the elective principle continued uninterruptedly from Vedic times to the Buddhistic Age 2."

Islam's social contract.

The theory of social contract was also known to the Muslim Jurists. The jurist Mawardi formulated a theory of bilateral contract between the nation and the sovereign. The Khalifa elect could refuse to take the responsibility but if he accepted it, then some of the important duties were :—

(1) To uphold the fundamental principles of Islam and to aid in the administration of the country.

(2) To defend the Muslim territories. Mawardi's political theory is supported by the inaugural address delivered by the First Khalifa of Islam, Abu Bakr. He spoke thus :

"After all praise to Almighty, O	اما بعد ايها الناس فوالله ما كنت حريصاً
people of God. I had no desire to	على الامارة يوما ولا ليلة قط ولا كنت راغباً فيها
become your leader at any time nor	ولا سالتها الله عز وجل فى سر وعلانية ولكني

1. A. C. Das, Rgvedic Culture, p. 298.

2. Ibid, p. 314.

did I pray God to confer upon me this honour, but I feared lest there should be some trouble. There is no comfort to me in being in office, instead such a burden has been put upon me that I can hardly bear it, I can go through it only by the help of God. It was my desire that the best of you should occupy this place, as it is I have been made your leader, and I am not 'the best of you.' If I go on the right path, help me, if I go astray, put me right ; the weaker amongst you is stronger in my eyes. I shall see by the grace of God that he secures his rights, and the aggressive among you is the weaker in my eyes I shall take away what is not his by right. A nation that gives up 'Jihad' is trodden upon, and a nation that becomes immoral is destroyed by God. So long as I follow God and his Apostle follow me and when I deviate in the minutest details from the law of God and the Prophet then you need obey me no more. Now rise for the prayers. May God have His mercy upon you."

اشفقت من الفتنة ولكن قلدت امرا عظيما مالي
به طاقة ولا يدان الا بتقوية الله عز و جل ولوددت
ان اقوى الناس عليها مكاني اليوم اني قد وليت
عليكم ولست بخيركم فان احسنت فاعينوني
وان اساءت فقوموني الصدق امانة والكذب
خيانة والضعيف فيكم قوي عندي حتى ازيح
عليه حقه انشاءالله والقوي منكم ضعيف حتى
اخذ الحق منه انشاءالله — لايدع قوم الجهاد
في سبيل الله الا ضربهم الله بالذل ولا يشيع الفاحشة
في قوم قط الا عمهم الله بالبلاء اطيعوني
ما اطعت الله رسوله فاذ اعصيت الله رسوله فلا
طاعة لي عليكم قوموا الى صلوتكم يرحمكم
الله تعالى —

Historical School.

Austin and Maine have severely criticised the theory of social contract and calls it a fiction on the ground that in primitive times the idea of contract was unknown, and that it neglects the fact that in early times the unit is not the individual but the family. In historical development of political society the idea of family was prominent it was superseded by the notion of kinship which was in turn replaced by the principle of local contiguity, as the basis of social organisation. The tribal chief was superseded by the military leader. When the military leader consolidated his position and power the institution became permanent and hereditary. This is the real origin of kingship.

Separation of Powers.

Montesquieu developed the theory of separation of powers. He started from the premises that the State is a manifestation of force; and there is a danger of abuse of power hence "to prevent this abuse, it is necessary from the very nature of things that power should be a check to power"[1]. The sovereign

---

1. De lesprit des lois LIV XI, ch IV.

authority should be broken in pieces and independent legislative executive, and judicial powers must be created. The need for the separation of power is felt, because the State is still considered as a Leviathan or monster which should be rendered harmless. The theory of separation of powers is also found in Islam. For a time the Prophet of Islam had combined the executive, judicial and legislative functions in his own person, however after the revelation of Koran the division became a necessity. The judiciary was the first to separate from the executive. Von Hammar says, "The Islamite administration, even in its infancy, proclaims in word and in deed the necessary separation between judicial and executive power."[1]

Popular Sovereignty and the theory of law.

Rousseau was the first to formulate the theory of popular sovereignty According to him the community is the State endowed with all rights and duties of sovereignty over its members. Hence every government is a "commission du peuple" and that the people's mandate is revocable at the will of the community, this general will is considered as positive law. However Rousseau like Hobbes and Locke clings to the theory of social contract, but for this Rousseau may be regarded as the originator of the moder n constitutional theory of the State. The modern King is simply an element of the constitution. The community and the sovereign are still opposed, but the community, as represented in the legislature is conceived as the supreme and permanent element in the constitution. The political sovereignty is undoubtedly vested in the electorate.

Laband had expressed himself thus, "that the State can require no performance and impose no restraint, can command its subjects in nothing and forbid them in nothing except on the basis of a legal prescription" The impersonal authority of the law as the supreme power is recognised. It is no longer held that the State subordinates itself to the law but that the authority of the State is nothing more than the authority of the law, that is the authority of the law and of the State are identical.

1. Ameer Ali. A History of the Saracens, p, 62.

S. Khuda Bukhsh says (contributions to the History of Islamic civilization p. 257) ", as early as Omar we have the administrative, the fiscal, the judiciary—the different branches of the Government are separate and distinct."

2. Staatsrecht des deutschen Reicht. Ed. 4. Vol. 11. p. 178.

The modern theory of law has its basis, in "the spiritual life of man" his feelings and his sense of right. Law is no more the will of the sovereign[1]. Coupled with this view the theory of popular sovereignty accords with the fundamental principles of the Muslim polity. "There is no government but God's "says the Koran "and Him alone is the Muslim to serve." Next to God the sovereign power resides in the people and Islamic law does not admit of "the sovereign power being dissociated from the people however they might choose to exercise it."[2]

Majority principle, Ijma.

The basis of the majority principle is the individual sense of right. It has been much criticised as it starts from "absolute individualism", and does not recognise "determination by objective norms," nor does it take into account the eternal laws. However the fact that a rule is accepted by the majority shows that it possesses a higher spiritual value, and as it is essential that there should be a single rule, the majority principle becomes an absolute necessity. The unwritten universal laws and legislation are also the outcome of an organised sense of right.

Ijma.

The majority principle is fully recognized in the Muslim polity. It is technically known as *Ijma* of the people. Its authority is based on well-known *Hadises.* "My followers will never agree upon what is not right." "It is incumbent upon you to follow the most numerous body." The contested election of the first Khalifa Abu Bakr was based on the *Ijma* of the people. The first, followers of Islam found the doctrine of *Ijma* as a suitable mode for deciding all important issues in matters of religion and temporal administration.[3] In the *Majlis Shura* the republican deli-

1. Professor H. Krabbe says (the modern idea of the State p 35) "We do not in the least deny that the notion of sovereignty has been justified ; we hold purely that among civilized peoples, it is now no longer recognised and that accordingly it must be expunged from political theory."

Ibid p 38. "So long as the authority of the sovereign was taken as the starting point, the basis of the authority was sought either in the will of God or in original social compact or compact with the sovereign, or in the natural power of the strong over the weak. The theory of the sovereignty of law, on the other hand takes account only of that basis for authority which it finds in the spiritual life of man, and specifically in that part of the spiritual life which operates in us as a feeling or sense of right."

2. Abdur Rahim Muhammadan Jurisprudence p. 60.

3. "In one of the oldest religio-political tracts Kitab-ul-Luma it is expressly stated that it is not permissible to hold that the entire community can commit an error of judgment," S. Khuda Buksh." The Orient under the Caliphs p. 259.

berative body important problems were decided by the majority of votes. Indeed the application of *Ijma* is the referendum of the Muslim polity.

It cannot be said that the theory of representation was totally unknown to the Arabs, even prior to Islam they had a tribal council which was composed of the family heads more or less on representative lines. It is an irony of fate that the Arabs could not reconcile *Ijma* universal sufferage—with the progressive requirements of their democratic constitution of the Khilafat. Hence when Monarchy was established the idea of *Ijma* was completely changed. Another republican idea was abandoned. The *Ijma* of the people was converted into the *Ijma* of the jurists, the argument was that the *Ijma* of the people to be co-extensive with the limits of the empire was an impossibility, hence its scope was narrowed down to the learned jurists as representatives of the entire Muslim world. It is in this capacity that the *ulema* elected the Ottoman Sultans as Khalifa of Islam.

The jurists Mawardi maintained, that in theory the right of electing a Khalifa belongs to the entire empire, though in practice only the inhabitants of the capital participated in the election of the Khalifa. Other jurists definitely maintained that the election was only valid, when the entire electorate of the empire had taken part—a perfect universal sufferage.[2]

Turning now to the *Ijma* of the jurists the republican flexibility of the rule is still maintained. It is recognized that *Ijma* may be reversed by the subsequent *Ijma* of the jurists.

---

1. The Ottoman Sultan was likewise deposed only on the sanction of the Sheik-ul-Islam as representative of the *ulema*.

2. S. Khuda Buksh. The Orient under the Caliphs p. 265.

X

THE INSTITUTION OF KHILAFAT

Khilafat.

The idea of hereditary kingship or of divine consecration was unknown to the first followers of Islam. Among the ancient Arabs the chief of the tribe owed his authority to general election, and he could also be deposed at the will of the people. On the death of the Prophet A. D 632 Abu Bakr was elected the first Khalifa by a general election, thereby establishing the old Arabian principle of free election.[1] On the next day the people swore allegiance to the first Khalifa of Islam. On his death in A. D. 634 'Umar became the second Khalifa. His election for confirmation caused no excitement as he was nominated by Abu Bakr as his successor. This incident serves as a precedent that a Khalifa was deemed to possess the right to nominate, provided his nominee was confirmed in his position by the people. 'Umar while on his death bed (A. D 644) appointed a council of regency including his son Abdur Rahman but with condition that on no account was 'Abdur Rahman to set himself up as a candidate for the Khilafat; thereby repudiating the doctrine of hereditary succession. Usman was elected as the third Khalifa and on his death A. D. 655, Ali was elected as the fourth Khalifa The reign of Ali is marked with the first two civil wars of Islam. Ali was victorious at the battle of Camel A. D. 666, but the struggle against Muawiyah the Governor of Syria was indecisive[3]. After the assassination of Ali Muawiyah consolidated his position, the Khilafat passed into his hands, and he established the Umayyad dynasty. The capital of Islam was removed from Medina to Damascus.

The era of the "rightly guided Khalifas" and the republican period came to an end with Ali. The administrative machinery of the government was simple. The Khalifa was not vested with any legislative powers. He was bound like any other person by the laws of Islam. His

---

1. Referring to this incident Macdonald says (Development of Muslim theology, etc. p 18). "The scene as it can be put together from Arabic historians, is curiously suggestive of the methods of modern politics."

2. The council consisted of Usman, Ali, Zubayr, Talha, Sa'd, Abdur-Rahman Ibn Awf and Abdur-Rahman Ibn Umar.

8. The majority of the first followers of Islam supported Ali and it is stated that in the battle of *Siffin* 2800 companions of the Prophet fought on behalf of Ali. This period also marks the division between the Muslims into the Orthodox school, the Sunni [illegible] Shia [illegible] Kharijiets.

policy was dictated by the famous republican assembly known as Majlis-i-shura[1]. The second Khalifa Umar himself declared, "the institution[2] of Khilafat is void without the deliberative council" لا خلافة الا عن مشورة

Maulana Shibli mentions another deliberative body which was subordinate to the Majlis-i-shura where ordinary problems of administration were discussed. The provincial administration was thoroughly democratic. Umar even gave powers to the provinces to elect their own governors whose appointments were then confirmed by the Khalifa. For instance, Usman bin Farqa, Hajjaj bin Alat and Man bin Yazid were selected by the inhabitants of Basra, Kufa and Sham (Syria), and their selection was accordingly confirmed by Umar.

The following were the chief administrative departments:—

(1) The Bait-ul-mal بیت المال the treasury.

(2) The Mahasil محاصل the Board of Taxes.

(3) The Jund جند the Military Department.

(4) The educational and religious instruction department.

(5) The Dar-ul-kuza and Ifta دارالقضاۃ ; افتا the judicial department.

(6) The Ahdas احداث the Police Department.

The Land policy during the reign of Khulafa-ur-rashidin was that of State-ownership. Umar had expressly prohibited the Arabs from acquiring land outside Arabia.[3] The Arabs were not permitted to follow agricultural pursuits. The Khalifa declared Sawad as an inalienable crown-land for all time, and all its revenue was utilised for the benefit of the State. The Military[4] organisation of the Arabs was far superior to their neighbouring States and they were fully acquainted with the Byzantine and the Persian art of warfare[5]. Von Kremer says, "Thus did Arabs establish their worldwide Empire on the solid and unchanging basis of human nature."

---

1. The well-known members of Majlis Shura were Usman, Ali, Abdur-Rrahman bin Awf, Muaz bin Jabal, Ubayy bin Kab and Zayd bin Sabit.

   The Koran Part 25, Ch. 42. و امرهم شوری بینهم

2. Al faruq p. 136.

3. Khalifa III Usman did not strictly adhered to this policy. The Umayyad king Umar II again prohibited Muslims from acquiring landed property.

4. S. Khuda Buksh. The Orient under the Caliphs, p. 305.

5. Shibli. Al faruq الفاروق p. 172.

MONARCHY IN ISLAM

Kingship. It has been observed that politics and religion according to the Semitic conception were more or less identical and synonymous. The institution of Khilafat bears both a spiritual and temporal character. The Arabs in addressing the Khalifa used the word Imam[1] which signifies the leader of prayers in the mosque. Out of the Imamate the idea of sovereignty and kingship took its root. The later Muslim jurists who have philosophically dealt with the theory of Sovereignty point out monarchy as a necessary institution, and further "according to their view kingship was an indispensable condition precedent to civilisation."

The Umayyads themselves recognised that a change had come in the nature of the Islámic Empire, in fact Muawiyah openly said that he was the first king of Islam. The democratic principles of Islam were trampled down, and instead absolute Sovereignty came into existence.

The Umayyad dynasty was thrown over by the Abbasides (in A. D. 749) who ruled the Muslim Empire for the next five centuries. The Muslims of Spain who were originally under the Umayyads, passed under the rule of the fugitive prince Abdur Rahman, who declared himself Khalifa of Islam also. In the meanwhile the Fatimids Khilafat as rival to the Abbasides had come into existence in Egypt, it was destroyed by Sultan Saladin. In A. D. 1258, the Abbaside Empire was shattered by the great conqueror Hulaku Khan, and the last of the Abbaside took refuge in Egypt, he continued to be recognised as the spiritual Imam and Khalifa in all its old glory, till Sultan Salim obtained in his favour renunciation of the office of Khilafat. Thereafter the Ottoman Sultans were recognised as the lawful Khalifas of Islam. The institution of Khilafat has ceased to exist since the deposition of the last Ottoman Khalifa Abdul Majid by the National Assembly of Angora.[2]

The theory of election The traditional custom of electing a Khalifa was reduced to mere formality, nevertheless sometimes the ceremony was performed in all its old glory. Here is an interesting sketch depicted by Von Kremer. "The only and exclusive source of Sovereignty and power was election by the assembled community of

---

1. Abu Bakr was called successor to the Prophet خليفة رسول الله but 'Umar respectfully declined to take this title, saying that he was unfit for this honour and he was content to be called Imam and also Amir-ul-muminin. امير المومنين 2. March 1924.

Muslims......the successor to the throne went to the chief mosque.... ascended the pulpit and delivered his inaugural address, which was followed by election and homage. On such an occasion the Omayyad Caliphs appeared dressed completely in white. The Abbasides were clad in black ......on such occasions the Caliph was decked with the insignia of Sovereignty"[1] "For deposing a Sovereign the people generally met in the chief mosque. Some man of position addressed the assembly when charges were formulated and made against the ruling Caliph and his deposition was declared in the interest of Islam"[2]. Later on election and homage was paid in a great State-Assembly in the presence of State officials and judges. When the Umayyads succeeded in establishing an equally glorious dynasty in Spain, they transplanted at the Court of Cordova the characteristic principles of pomp and magnificence of Damascus. The spectacle at Cordova was equally majestic.

The Ottoman Sultans also preserved the idea of free election. Each new Sultan was solemnly elected by the Ulema and divines of Constantinople, and they acted in the capacity of representatives of the Muslims. Thus the theoretical position though it has been modified still maintains the broad characteristic of free election[3]. However the succession to kingship was not altogether hereditary. It is true that first Muslim King Muawiyah secured succession for his son, but out of the fourteen rulers of the Umayyad dynasty only four had their sons as successors, and all of them (even though it be nominally) were elected.

The cases of a minor being elected are very rare, for instance when Muqtadir was to be elected the Kazi, Musanna refused to elect and pay homage to him. He observed, "I would not elect a boy to be a Khalifa"[4]. This firm attitude cost him his life. As regards the Ottomans kingship was not absolutely hereditary, the eldest son usually did not succeed. The Sultan's successor was the eldest and fittest member of the royal family.

During the reign of the Umayyads the following were the chief offices:—

(1) The *Diwan-ul-Khiraj* the board of land tax which was in the nature of the Department of Finance. (2) The *Diwan-ul-Khitam*

1. S. Khuda Buksh the Orient under the Caliphs p. 252.

2. Ibid p. 268.

3. The orthodox view that the Quraish are only eligible for the office of Khalifa has never been accepted by the Muslim world. The Shia on the other hand confine eligibility for the office of Khalifa to the House of Ali only.

4. S. Khuda Bukhsh the Orient under the caliphs p. 257.

the Board of the Signet, the ordinances after being sealed were issued. (3) The *Diwan-ur-Rasail* the Board of correspondence. (4) The *Diwan-ul-Mustaghillat*, The Board of Revenue. (5) The *Nazir-ul-Mazalim* the judiciary. Every province had a Governor, a Kazi and a police officer.

The Abbasides were the first to create the office of Wizarat (Prime Minister), it is admittedly of the Persian origin. When the Buwayyid Sultan had virtually taken the Khalifa under their tutelage the office of Wizarat came more into prominence. There were two kinds of Wizarat, (1) unlimited, (2) limited. The Wazir with unlimited powers was called the Grand Wazir. He practically exercised the prerogatives of the Sultan without preliminary sanction while it was necessary for the limited Wazir to obtain Sultan's sanction for his administrative acts.

The Governorship of the provinces was also divided into unlimited and limited ones like the Wizarat. They exercised only temporal powers. It should be noted that the Governors appointed by the Khulfa-ur-rashidun occupied different position, they were the representatives of the Khalifa in not mearly administrative, military, financial and judicial matters but also in all spiritual and religious matters of Islam.

During the reign of the Abbasides the following were the chief offices :—

(1) The *Diwan-ul-Khiraj*, the Board of Taxes.

(2) The *Diwan-ul-Dhiyya'*, the Board of the Crown lands.

(3) The *Diwan-ul-Zamimah*, the Board of Accounts.

(4) The *Diwan-ul-Jund Wal Shaqiriyyah*, the Military Board.

(5) The *Diwan-ul Barid*, the Post office Board.

(6) The *Diwan Zimam Wa Nafaqat* the Board of General expenditure.

(7) The *Nazir-ul Mazalim* the Board for the administration of Justice.

The recent Ottoman Sultans had a cabinet of ministers almost of modern type with the exception of the Sheikh-ul-Islam who occupied a unique position and shared in "the spiritual life" of the Khalifa. The following are the four chief offices as found in the Qanun Namah, the fundamental laws of the Turks[1]. (1) The Wazir, (2) The Kazi Asker the Military judge, (3) The Defeder, the Finance Minister, (4) and the Nichandji the secretary.

1. Sir E. Creasy, History of the Ottoman Turks, p. 158,
" The dome of the State is supported by four pillars"

Fifty years after the dawn of Islam, kingship was established all over the Muslim world. It is true that some of the Muslim Kings of the Umayyad dynasty like Yazid I, Walid II and Marwan III or of those of the Abbaside dynasty like Mustanjid and Muqtadir discredited Islam; but such reigns cannot cast a melancholy shadow on the splendour and glory of the reigns of Umar bin Abdul Aziz or Mansur or Harun and Mamun. The great potentates of the Umayyads and Abbasides and those of the Ottomans like Muhammad II and Salim compared favourably with the greatest of the ruling dynasties known to the world.[1] The Umayyads of Spain were equally renowned for their rule.

Sovereignty of law.

The most autocratic of the Muslim King cannot be regarded in the domain of law as an omnipotent sovereign answering the Austinian definition. A Muslim sovereign is bound by the sacred law of Islam[2]. The Islamic code stands supreme. The Muslim kings have usually themselves refrained from asserting their authority so as to mould the sacred law. The Ulema and Mujtahids have always exercised a tremendous influence over the people, and have served as checks on the royal prerogatives. Acknowledgment of God's authority and His right to issue commands is embedded in our constitution.[3] The sovereignty of law in Islam is unchallengable. The end of law in every legal system is to promote the welfare of men, but the conception of the Muslim law goes further; the welfare of men is not merely in respect of life on this earth, but also of future life, so that imperishability of human

---

1. The Islamic culture was at once brilliant and varied In philosophy, astronomy, Medicine, Surgery, Mathematics, Physics, Chemistry, Architecture manufacture and trade the Muslims were the pioneer. The works of Socrates, Plato and Aristotle were critically studied and new results were arrived at by Ibn Rushd (Avirtoes' Abu Ali Sina (Avicenna) and al Farabi. Ibn Rushd was also an astronomer. Abul Hasan (Abhazen) was a great physicist. Jabir (Geber) is recognised as the Patriarch of Chemistry. Amir Yaqub is credited with the invention of artillery. The Muslim architecture is famous all over the world. The Arabs were great traders. The poetical works of Sadi, Jami, Umar, Khayyam and Hafiz are appreciated throughout the world. The Muslim Jurisprudence was greatly developed by jurists like Imam Jafar, Abu Hanifa, Shafii, Malik and Hanbal and their followers.

2. J. Bryce admits this ('Studies in History and Jurisprudence' p. 90) he says "In all Muhammedan countries the monarch is legally, as well as practically, restrained by his inability to change the sacred Law."

3. The theory of some jurists is that the origin of law is to be found in a primordial covenant (ميثاق ازل) entered into between God and man, the other jurists regard this covenant to be an allegory.

life is another postulate underlying the Islamic conception of the law. The Muslim law is "fundamentally democratic and opposed in essence to absolutism."[1] It is presumed that every Muslim in Dar-ul-Islam knows the laws of the land. To this extent the maxim "Ignorantia juris non excusat" applies to the Muslim law.[2]

"When the law is promulgated in Dar-ul-Islam, the mission of the law-giver is complete, and a person who remains ignorant of the law, is due to his own negligence and not to the non-publicity of the law and hence his ignorance is not excusable"

اصول بزدوی حاشیه کشف

فاما اذا انتشر الخطاب في دار الاسلام فقد
تم التبليغ من صاحب الشرع فمن جهل من بعد
فانما اتى من قبل تقصيره لا من قبل خفاء الدليل
فلا يعذر -

Conclusion.

The conception of the Muslim State is the institution of Khilafat as the supreme executive This idea was translated into facts, it was realised only for a short period during the Khilafat of Khulafa-ur-rashidun and then vanished from the angle of vision of the Muslims. Sir William Muir observed, "The Caliphate ended with the fall of Bagdad. The illusory resuscitation by the Memluks was a lifeless show; the Osmanli Caliphate a dream[3] and "that while the Umeivad Caliphate from first to last, was co-ordinate with the limits of Islam, this is no longer true of the Abbasid"[4]. In my opinion the real Islamic institution of Khilafat—which is the admiration of the world and the pride of the Muslims—perished with the first followers of Islam, it has ever since been a dream. But the Muslim ideals are imperishable they stand out to day in all their ancient splendour as testimony to the Golden age of Islam. They are our heritage not for adoration and worship, but to be followed by acts and precepts to achieve a new era for mankind Islam stands for the welfare of humanity. Vambery has well depicted the scene, "It is not", he says, "Islam and its doctrines which have devastated the western portion of Asia and brought about the present sad state of things, but it is the tyranny of the Muslim princes who have wilfully perverted the doctrines of the Prophet. . . . and efficaciously distorting and crushing all liberal principles they have prevented the dawn of a Moslem Renaissance"[5].

---

1. A. H. Lybyer "the Turkish Parliament" Proceedings of the American Political science Association Vol. vii P. 67.
2. Ignorance of fact is in some cases a ground for exemption under the Muslim law.
3. Sir William Muir The Caliphate p. 596.
4. Ibid p. 432.
5. Western culture in Eastern Lands p. 357. Dr. L. Stoddard in his book the New World of Islam argues in favour of the Muhammadan Revival.

JUSTICE

The first essential function of the State is to administer justice, maintain peace and internal order. To establish justice must be one of the great ends of every civilised government. Even in arbitrary government it serves as security against popular cruelty and private vengeance. The protection of the " weak " against " the strong " is not the sole function of justice. It should also be able to safeguard the interest of society against wrong doers.

Civilisation stands for the betterment and progress of humanity; its basis is perfect administration of justice. In short justice is the basis of all institutions of the State. It is the foundation of public peace and national prosperity. The Muslim notion of the administration of justice is stated in the Holy Koran.

" Surely we have revealed the Book to you with the truth that you may judge between people by means of that which Allah has taught you."

Part V Ch IV

انا انزلنا اليک الکتاب بالحق لتحکم بين الناس
بما اراک الله

" O you who believe, be maintainers of justice, bearers of witness for Allah's sake though it may be against your ownselvesor your parents or near relatives. If he be rich or poor, Allah is most competent to deal with them both, therefore do not follow your low desires lest you deviate, and if you swerve or turn aside then surely Allah is aware of what you do."

يا يها الذين آمنوا کونوا قوامين بالقسط شهداء
لله ولو على انفسکم او الوالدين والاقربين ان
يکن غنيا او فقيرا فالله اولى بهما . فلا تتبعوا
الهوى ان تعدلوا و ان تلوا او تعرضوا فان الله
کان بما تعملون خبيرا

The administration of justice is guided by two agencies - the substantive code and the legal procedure. Historically th law of Procedure is the basis of the substantive law. The Procedure by decided case reveals who shall be protected and the matters on which protection shall be granted. These revelations are the foundation of the Substantive Law[1]. The State is the custodian of law and order. In every country justice is administered in the King's name, the judges are appointed by the executive power and hold office during good behaviour. Bentham however contends for the opposite view. He says "The fountain of justice is the nation through the channel of the legislature. Justice shall not be administered in the name of the king or any other single person", and "the judges shall in general be elected by the persons subject to their jurisdiction"[2] No country has accepted Bentham's democratic ideals in entirety. We shall consider them again in connection with the United States of America and the theory of the Muslim Administration of Justice.

Ancient Society.

In ancient society the king was usually associated with the administration of justice. He was also the chief military leader. The Homeric king was usually busy with fighting and he administered divine justice. The Hebrew judges also represent an old form of kingship. While Saul and David are famous as military kings Solomon is known as a judicial king. The famous Hundred Court which administered the Salic Law to the Salian ranks had at first an elective President named Thunginus or Thingman[3]. After a while this popular head disappeared, and he was succeeded by a deputy of the king called the Graf or Count. Thus Royal authority displaced the popular control. Similarly the feudal theory is based on the assumption that the king alone is to administer Justice

1. The law of Civil Procedure forms an integral part of the codification of Roman law by Justinian. The Napoleonic codification classified the law of Procedure in a separate Code and thisl example has been followed by Germany, Italy, Belgium, Japan and India.

2. J. Bentham Art. I and Art. II Draught for the organization of Judicial Establishments.

3. Sir Henry Maine "Early law and custom" p. 170.

The Hindu Law expresses the need for the administration of justice thus: "Virtue having become extinct among men, judicial procedure has been established and the king having the privilege of inflicting punishments, has been instituted judge of law suits."[1]

The Hindu Theory.

In the Hindu theory of the administration of justice "the king is the fountain-head of justice[2], though Brihaspati says "A Brahmana is the root of the tree of justice; the sovereign prince is its stem and branches; the ministers are its leaves and blossoms; and just government is its fruit (1·34.)" Brihaspati's conception of Justice and kingship was apparently not developed by the Hindu jurists, and the credited theory of "divine right" was in favour of the king to be the fountain of of justice. But there is one remarkable difference between the feudal and the Hindu theory. In the feudal society whereas the king himself at first administered justice, it is not so in the Hindu society[3].

According to the Sukraniti the king was never to try cases alone and the same view is expressed in the Yajanavalkya. Brihaspati clearly differentiates between the functions of the king and the judges. He says, "The Chief Justice decides causes: the King inficts punishments: the judges investigate the merits of the case"[4], Narada likewise observes "Attending to the dictates of the law book and adhering to the opinion of his Chief Justice let him (*i. e.* the king) try causes in due order"[5] The king together with the Chief Justice, Pradvivaka, and other judges dharmukah formed the Supreme Court.[6]

---

1. Ganganatha Jha "Studies in Hindu Law" p. 1.
2. Narada (Jolly) Legal Procedure III. 7.
3. G. Buhler, the Laws of Manu VIII, 8, & 9. p. 254.

Manu says, "Depending on the eternal law, let him decide the suits of men", and again, "But if the king does not personally investigate the suits, then let him appoint a learned Brahmana to try them."

4. Brihaspati 1·6 5 Narada (Jolly) Legal Procedure p. 35

6. P. Banerjea Public Administration in Ancient India p. 143. "It was the Chief Justice who in reality presided ever the Kings courts, even when the King was present"

The language of the law books employs the word king as doing all matters of legal execution. Justice is administered in the king s name. This accords with the theory of divine right, and hence some consider that the king is above the law. However Mr. Jayswal definitely holds that "even in the palmiest days of Hindu Monarchy neither in the Manava Dharmasastra nor in the Artha-Sastra was the king placed above the law."[1] The king appoints judges and may dismiss them.

United Kingdom.

In the United Kingdom the king is over all persons in all causes as well in ecclesiastical as civil within his dominions supreme. This idea is a remnant of feudalism. The king at first himself administered justice, and later on the judges were called on to his assistance, and they made use of the king's name.

The administration of justice has always been centralised in England. The House of Lords is in fact as well as in form the Supreme Court of Appeal in England, though in practice it has ceased to exercise its judicial functions which are now exercised by the Lord Chancellor and "special law Lords"—Lords of Appeal in Ordinary.

The British Supreme Court of Judicature is composed of the High Court and the Court of Appeal. The High Court of Justice has three divisions—the Chancery division, the Kings Bench division and a Probate, Divorce and Admiralty division. From these appeal lies to the court of Appeal and thence to the House of Lords. The Judicial Committee of the Privy Council generally hears Appeals from India and the Colonies. The Judges of the Supreme Court "save the Chancellor are appointed by Letters Patent under the great seal on the advice of the Chancellor"[2] They are required to take the judicial oath and they hold office during good behaviour, and they can only be removed on address of both Houses of Parliament. Thus the nation exercises influence on the judiciary through the medium

---

1. Hindu Polity II p. 152.

2. W. R. Anson Law and Custom of the Constitution. Vol. II p. 268.

of its representatives in Parliament. The holding of any office under the Crown is not affected by the demise of the Crown [1].

Austin denies that a sovereign could be legally bound, if it could it would no longer be sovereign. Indeed this is true of the sovereign body in the United Kingdom. De Lolme has summed up this doctrine thus that the British "Parliament can do everything but make a woman a man and a man a woman."

The English courts are not to determine whether an Act of Parliament is immoral or invalid because it went beyond the limits of Parliamentary authority. The British Parliament is supreme, it is a sovereign legislature.[2]

France.

The supreme court of France is the Cassation Court which sits at Paris. Next to it are several Courts of Appeal which hear cases coming from the courts of first instance of the districts. The President of the Republic appoints judges in consultation with the Minister of Justice, and the judges hold office during good behaviour. The administrative courts determine questions affecting the State. In France there is a distinction between Public Law which concerns the government and Private Law which deals with the relations of individuals to one another. The highest administrative court is the Council of State which is composed of ministers and officials. Subordinate to the Council of State there are the Praefectural Council, a Court of Revision, a Superior Council of Public Instruction and a Court of Audit. To coordinate the working of this double system there is a court known as the Tribunal of Conflicts.

Germany.

The supreme Court of Germany is known as Reichsgericht. In each province there are two courts Oberlandesgericht and Landgericht; in each district there is an Amtsgericht, the court of first instance. The judges are

---

1. The demise of the Crown Act 1 Ed. VII. c 5.

2. A. V. Dicey Law of the Constitution p 58 "English judges do not claim or exercise any power to repeal a statute."

nominated by the executive power, and their appointment is for life, and thus the independence of the judiciary is secured.

The administrative courts, Verwaltungsgerichte similar to the French administrative courts tries cases arising out of the exercise of the States sovereignty, e-g the case of an alleged unlawful action on the part of an official. Similar to France the Court of Conflicts (Gerichtshof fur Kompetenz knonflikte) sits to determine the jurisdiction of the ordinary and administrative courts. The supreme administrative court Oberverwaltungsgericht, sits in Berlin, it has the same footing as the Reichsgericht, This distinction in ordinary courts of justice and administrative does not exist in England or the United States of America. The Minister of Justice controls all criminal prosecutions.

The United States of America.

Lord Bryce has described the United States, as a "Commonwealth of commonwealths, a Republic of republics, State which, while one, is nevertheless composed of other States even more essential to its existence than it is to theirs.[1]" The American political institutions are in the main the political institutions of England adapted to the requirements of an "ultra democratic" constitution. In U. S. A. sovereignty is really divided between a sovereign legislature, a sovereign executive and a sovereign judicature.[2]

The administration of justice is carried out by the State Courts and the Federal Judiciary. The State courts are in no sense organs of federal justice as the courts in Germany are,[3] they

1. American Commonwealth Vol. 1 p. 15

2. Austin holds that this distinction is not precise, he says in the United States "the sovereignty of each of the States and also of the larger State arising from the federal union resides in the States' govervmeents as forming one aggregate body" Austin based his view on article V of the constitution which requires the consent of three fourths of the State Legislatures for any amendment in the Constitution, yet this very article V provides that certain portions of the Constitution shall be unalterable till 1808, and further it provides that no State shall be deprived of its equal suffrage in the Senate without its own consent."

3. W. Wilson The State p. 491

exercise independent local jurisdiction. Every State has its supreme court and its subordinate tribunals. The supreme courts exercise appellate jurisdiction. In most of the States the judges are elected by the people, in some by the legislature, and in some they are appointed by the Governor with the advice and consent of the Senate. The supreme court judges are also elected by the people. The terms of the judges vary from two years to a tenure during good behaviour. The judges may be removed by the legislature and in some States by the governor at the request of the legislature. Thus we see that Bentham's idea of judges being elected by the people has found favour in some of the States in America.

The Federal judiciary consists of a Supreme court, Circuit courts of appeal, Circuit courts and District courts and a Court of claims. The authority of the federal judiciary is based on the Constitution which defines and limits its jurisdiction. The Federal Judges are appointed by the President with the consent and advice of the Senate. They hold office during good behaviour The federal judiciary is the custodian of the American Constitution By Article VI, the Constitution itself together with laws and treaties made in conformity with it was made "The Supreme Law of the Land", and the judges are bound by them not only as against the State laws but also against State Constitutions. Hence the framers of the constitution meant that it was not only for the judges to interpret the statute law, but also to determine, whether it was in harmony with "the higher law" embodied in the constitution.[1]

Muslin Theory

In the Muslim theory of administration of Justice the fountain head is not the Khalifa, Sultan or King, but "The entire Moslem community is responsible

---

1. Greene E. B. the Foundations of American Nationality, p. 595.

"The idea of checks and balances' runs through the whole work of the convention. The executive is checked by the Senate in the matter of treaties and appointments. The Legislative department is checked by its division into two houses and by the President's veto which was finally agreed upon instead of giving this power to 'a council of revision' composed of the Executive and the Judges. Even more important perhaps was the 'check imposed upon both these departments through the judiciary."

for the administration of Justice"[1] The fountain head of Justice is the Koran and the legislative sovereignty is vested in the people. Justice is administered in Gods name[2]. Any Muslim[3], who is adult, sane, free[4], of irreproachable character, sound of hearing, sight[5] and speech; educated and having knowledge of Shara both theoretical and practical, may be appointed to the office of a judge. However the sovereign may orally or in writing appoint judges. The extent of the Judge's jurisdiction must be specified. The Sultan may lawfully appoint judges for a particular time or for a certain kind of proceedings. According to the Shafii Law an appointment of a judge by the sovereign should be drawn up in writing and must be before two witnesses.

The power for the appointment of judges is exclusively vested in the sovereign power. This power cannot be exercised by the people of any particular locality, and if the inhabitants of a place assemble and elect a judge, he shall not be considered as a lawful judge[6]. However the Sovereign may delegate the power of appointment to the Governors or to the Kazi-ul-Kuzat, the Chief Kazi. The death of the Sovereign does not *ipso facto* involve the dismissal of the judiciary. The judges continue to discharge their functions. Accordingly the Fatawa Alamgiri says.

Even after the Sultan's death the Kazis appointed by him will continue to discharge their duties.	فتاوی عالمگیری و اذا مات الخليفة وله قضاة (ج٣) فهم على حالهم

1. Minhaj et Talibin by Mahiuddin Abu Zakaria Yahya ibn Sharif en Nawawi, p. 500. (translated by L. W. C. Van Den Berg and E. C. Howard)

2. After the republican age of Islam this conception was replaced by the doctrine that sovereign is the fountain of justice. See the chapters on the Administration of Justice of the Muslim Law in Turkey, in Persia and in India.

3. Non-Muslims are thus excluded from exercising authority over the Muslims.

4. The slaves are thus debarred.

5. According to Imam Malik blindness is not a ground for exclusion.

6 اجتمع اهل بلدة على رجل و جعلوه قاضيا يقضي في ما بينهم لا يصير قاضيا . فتاوی عالمگیری

According to Imam Abu Hanifa a woman is competent to exercise the functions of a judge in cases in which her testimony is legally admissible, while Abu Jarir Tabari maintains that a woman is a fit and proper person to administer justice in all cases.

Every system for the administration of justice emphasizes the need for publicity of Judicial proceedings. It is secured by means of having public law courts, and public oral proceedings. Until recently all proceedings in the Prussian Courts were written, they were finally replaced by public oral proceedings. The Muslim law has always insisted on public oral proceedings, in fact writing is not necessary in any legal transaction. According to the Hanafi system it is desirable to set apart a public building, *Dar-ul-Kuza*, for the administration of justice, and public Mosques could also be used as Law courts, but under the Shafii law it is forbidden to hold sittings in a mosque [1].

Bentham had expressed a hope that justice should be administered gratis, and that no stamp-duties or other duties should be leviable on judicial proceedings.[2] The above view is in complete harmony with the Muslim theory. There are no duties leviable in Islam. There are no stamps or court fees. Justice is administered gratis.

---

1. Minhaj et Talibin P. 504
2. J. Bentham Art IV (Draught for the organisation of judicial Establishments.)

" Justice shall be administered gratis. . . ." and Art V "All stamp duties or other duties upon law proceedings are hereby abolished."

II

THE ADMINISTRATION OF JUSTICE IN ARABIA

Ancient Arabia

The ancient Arabian nomadic confederation was the result of association of various tribes ; there was no State in the modern sense, or a settled form of Government for the administration of justice. The government was constructed on customary usages, and the administration of justice was carried on according to ancient customs. The tribal council did not make law. " The evolution of private law out of the State would be a contradiction of all history." The council applied and upheld the immemorial customs, assisted by the moral force of tribal opinion. The punishments were severe, it was customary to cut off the hands of thieves, to stone adulterers and adulteresses or to flog them after blackening their faces, and to demand blood money as compensation for minor injuries.

Oaths were administered for settling disputes, and for offences committed by a member of one tribe against the other it was usual to administer the sacred Oath in the *Hatim* of the Kaba. The laws regulating the relations of the sexes and inheritance were indefinite and vague. Polyandry, polygamy, marriage by capture, illicit connections and temporary marriages were all prevalent in ancient Arabia[1] There were no definite laws for causing separation. Divorce was very common and it was of various kinds [2]. These immemorial usages and customs form an integral part of the history of Muslim Jurisprudence. Islam only repealed such customary laws as were inconsistent with the principles of sound reason and good conscience. A custom which was immemorial, reasonable, continuous, certain and consistent with the Koranic injunctions is a part of the Muslim Law.[3]

---

1. The Muslim Law of Marriage by the present author pp. I—XV.
2. Ibid p. 66.
3. The Fatawa Kazi Khan says, "that which is established by custom is also regarded as established by the Law." فتاوى قاضي خان [illegible]
الثابت عرفا كالثابت شرعا

11

The Muslim Law.

The Legislative period of Islam.

The Koran may well be described as the final and the great legislative code of Islam, but the main object of the Koran was not promulgation of law, it simply laid down fundamental rules. The characteristic of the Islamic law is the complete identification of its origin with the personality of the great Arabian Prophet. Sir William Muir observes, "And so true a mirror is the Coran of Mahomet s character, that the saying became proverbial ... His character is the Coran."[1] Thus it can be said of the Prophet that he was not only the true founder of the Islamic religion, but the executive, judicial and legislative head of Islam on all points on which the Koran made no provisions. Every act of the Prophet was considered as *sunnat*, traditions, and wherever the Koran was silent, his decision was law, and as such the *hadises* rank as the next important source of Muhammadan law. The decisions of the Prophet of Islam are remarkable for their simplicity, fairness and equanimity. The Prophet confesses that he decides the case on evidence and is liable to err in forming his judgment like other human beings. An *Hadis* is reported in the Muslim :—

"It is reported from Umm Salmah that the Prophet of God said "you bring cases before me for my decisions and one of you tenders better proofs than the other, and I decide it accordingly on the evidence; but to those in whose favour I give judgment concerning any of the rights of his brother, let him not take it, for I only cut off for him a piece of the fire."

مسلم

عن ام سلمة رضي الله عنها قالت قال رسول الله
صلى الله عليه وسلم انكم تختصمون الى و لعل
بعضكم ان يكون الحن بحجته من بعض فاقضي
له على نحو مما اسمع منه فمن قطعت له من
حق اخيه شيئا فلا ياخذه فانما اقطع له به
قطعة من النار

1. The Life of Mahomet P. 563.

It is related by Ibn Abbas that "the Prophet said 'If men were given according to their claims then they would certainly lay claim to the blood of men as well as their property ; but an oath is incumbent upon the defendant."

مسلم

عن ابن عباس رضي الله تعالى عنهما ان النبي
صلى الله عليه وسلم قال لو يعطى الناس بدعو
اهم لا ادعى ناس د ماء رجال و اموالهم و
لكن اليمين على المدعى عليه

Thus the rule of Muslim Law in its infancy was that the plaintiff must produce witnesses, and the defendant is to take oath. A natural question arises whether the evidence of one witness is sufficient? The Hedaya says, "The evidence required in a case of whoredom is that of four men, as has been ordained in the Koran.......... the other evidence required in other criminal cases is that of two men, according to the text of the Koran .... In all other cases. the evidence required is that of two men or of one man and two women whether the case relates to property, or to other rights, such as marriage, divorce, agency, executorship or the like"[2] Thus the Muslim Hanafi law insists that there must be more than one witness, however according to the following *Hadis*, and according to Imam Shafii and Malik the evidence of one witness coupled with the plaintiff's oath is sufficient.

"It is reported by Ibn 'Abbas that the Prophet decided a case on one witnesse's evidence and on an oath."

مسلم

عن ابن عباس رضي الله تعالى عنهما ان رسول
الله صل الله عليه وسلم قضى بيمين و شاهد –

It is incumbent upon every witness to give evidence and the Holy Koran commands, " Let no witnesses withhold their testimony when it is demanded from them."

---

1. W. Goldsack 'Selections from Muhammadan traditions p. 195.
2. C. Hamilton Hedaya Vol. II Book XXI p. 667.

The following cases will illustrate how justice was administered. Abdullah bin Sahl was murdered by the Jews of Khaybar. Muhesa the deceased's cousin filed a complaint before the Prophet, but as no eye-witness of the deed was produced, the Prophet did not interfere, but alloted 100 camels from the treasury, bait–ut–mal, as blood-money.[1]

Some cases.

When the Prophet was unable to decide the cases he used to receive divine messages which served as precedents, and laid down the law. Here is an illustration which speaks for itself.

It is reported by Jabir that a woman brought her two daughters before the Prophet and said, "Oh! Apostle of God these two are daughters of Sabit bin Qays who fell fighting at the battle of Uhad, their uncle has taken away all the property and has left nothing for them, and what O, Prophet do you decide, it is not possible to get them married without property".[2] The Prophet answered that God could alone decide this point. Thereafter this verse was revealed and accordingly the Prophet sent for the woman and the uncle and told him to give $\frac{2}{3}$ of the property to the two daughters and $\frac{1}{8}$ to the woman and to take himself whatever remains after distribution.[2]

ابو داؤد - الترمذی

عنه (جابر) رضی الله تعالی عنه قال جاءت
امراة بابنتيها لها فقالت يا رسول الله هاتان
بنتا ثابت بن قيس قتل معک يوم احد و قد
استفاء عمهما مالهما و ميراثهما كله فلم يدع
لهما مالاً الا اخذه فما ترى يا رسول الله فوالله
لا تنكحان ابداً الا ولهما مال فقال النبي صلى الله
عليه و آله وسلم يقضى الله في ذلک فنزلت
سورة النساء يوصيكم الله في اولادكم الاية فقال
رسول الله صلى الله عليه وسلم ادعو الى المراة
وصاحبها فقال لعمهما اعطهما الثلثين و اعط امهما
الثمن و ما بقي فهو لک

---

1. This case is reported in Sahih Bukhari and Nisai
2. Thus the customary rule of ancient Arabia, that the uncle is

Hilal bin Umayyah, came before the Prophet and accused his wife of adultery with Sharik bin Sahima, The Holy Prophet in accordance with the Koranic injunctions demanded him to produce four witnesses, or in the alternative to submit himself to receive the prescribed punishment of eighty stripes for slandering a chaste woman. At this Hilal exclaimed "I swear by God, I am truthful. God will send down an order, and save me from being flogged." Thereupon the following Koranic verse was revealed, which served as substitute for the hudd-uz-zina or specific punishment for adultery.

The Koran says : Part XVIII. Ch. XXIV.

"Those who accuse their wives, but have no witnesses, except their ownselves, then their evidence is to witness God four times that they are truthful and the fifth time that the curse of God be upon him, if they be liars."

والذين يرمون ازواجهم ولم يكن لهم شهداء
الا انفسهم فشهادة احدهم اربع شهادات بالله
انه لمن الصادقين والخامسة ان لعنة الله عليه
ان كان من الكاذبين -

At the same time the Koran allows the wife also an opportunity to rebut her husband's oath.

Part XVIII. Ch. XXIV.

"But it will avert the punishment from her, if she will testify by God four times that he is a liar, and the fifth time that the wrath of God be upon her, if he be truthful."

ويدرؤ عنها العذاب ان تشهد اربع شهادات بالله
انه لمن الكاذبين والخامسة ان غضب الله عليها
ان كان من الصادقين -

---

entitled to deceased brother's property was completely over-ruled. The shares under the Muslim law are as follows:—

Wife, $\frac{1}{8}=\frac{3}{24}$

2 daughters—$\frac{2}{3}=\frac{16}{24}$ i. e. $\frac{8}{24}$ each.

Uncle, the residue, $\frac{5}{24}$

Thereupon the Prophet allowed Hilal to take the oath, and his wife also took the oath, but she was greatly perturbed and staggered while she was taking the oath. She gave birth to a son who closely resembled Sharik, however she was not punished as the procedure of lian is a substitute for the prescribed punishment for adultery.[1]

Such instances were common during the era of the Holy Prophet, for instance at the battle of Khaybar the Prophet forbade *Muta*, temporary marriages which were common in ancient Arabia.

The Prophet had become so well known for deciding cases impartially that the Jews and other non-Muslims used to refer cases for his decisions, and he used to decide the cases according to their own laws. An interesting case between the Jews of Banu Nazir and Qurayza came before the Prophet. Banu Nazir asserted a custom that if a man of Banu Qurayza murdered a man of Nazir then he should he killed, but if a Nazir murdered a Qurayza then the blood money was fixed at 100 camels. The Prophet decided that according to the Jewish sacred laws there is equality among the Jews, and that sacred law is to be respected.

The Prophet of Islam never considered himself above the law, and by this own acts and precepts he established a great constitutional precedent, that the head of the State could be sued both as a private individual and also in his public capacity. The example set by the Prophet was followed by first four Khalifas of Islam also. These instances, when Islam was at its infancy, (at the same time at its zenith as far as democratic principles are concerned) not only established constitutional precedents of supreme importance; but gave that natural touch and strength to the Muslim judiciary

1. This Hadis is reported in Bukhari.

2. See the Surat-ul-Muminin the Koran Part XVIII Ch. XXIII

3. As reported in Abu Daud.

that even during the era of absolute monarchy and autocracy, the reverence for judiciary never totally disappeared. The most autocratic of the Muslim kings that flourished during the reigns of the Umayyad and Abbaside, or in Egypt or distant Spain or India, they all submitted even though it be nominally to the decisions of the judiciary. The last public utterance of the Prophet testifies to his love for justice, he made a public declaration to the effect that if he were indebted to anyone or misappropriated anyone's property or done some harm to his life or reputation then he was present there to pay his dues to whomsoever dmanded. The audience was amazed and in the whole assembly there was only one person who claimed some dirhams and was paid accordingly. [1]

Thus during the era of the Prophet, the Koran was the supreme law, and wherever it was silent the traditions of the Prophet supplemented the Islamic Shera.

The principle of *Ijma* was also the immediate source of law, and here is an **Hadis** which establishes the principle of *Ijtihad*, that is a judge when he is unable to decide a case finding no solution for it in the Koran or Hadis may rely on his own private judgment *Ijtihad* is more elastic than any other judicial process known to the Muslim law. This famous Hadis is reported in Abu Daud and also in Tirmizi.

" It is related by the Ashab of Muaz bin Jabal that when the Apostle of God sent Muaz to Yemen, he said, "How will thou execute judgment when a case comes before thee, Muaz replied" I will judge by the Koran (book of God) Prophet said, "And if thou do not find (a

ابو داؤد

عن اصحاب معاذ بن جبل ان رسول الله
صلى الله عليه وسلم لما اراد ان يبعث معاذاً
الى اليمن قال كيف تقضى اذا عرض لك قضاء
قال اقضى بكتاب الله قال فان لم تجد فى
كتاب الله قال فبسنة رسول الله صلى الله عليه
وسلم قال فان لم تجد في سنة رسول الله
صلى الله عليه وسلم ولا فى كتاب الله قال

---

1. Maulana Shibli, Syrat-un-nabi on the authority of Ibn Ishaq. Vol II P. 245.

solution) in the book of God. Muaz replied ' Then (I will decide) in accordance with the traditions of the Prophet." The Prophet said " And if

اجتهد برأئى ولا آلو فضرب رسول الله صلى الله
عليه وسلم صدره قال الحمد لله الذي وفق رسول
الله صلى الله عليه وسلم لما يرضي رسول الله
صلى الله عليه وسلم .

thou do not find a similar case in the traditions ?", Muaz replied "Then I will decide according to my own judgment and will not slacken effort." Thereupon the Prophet smote upon his breast and said "Praise be to God who has caused the messenger of the Apostle of God to agree with what the Apostle of God likes."

The principle of *Ijtihad* is of supreme importance. Its application was absolutely necessary to develop the Muslim law and to administer justice equitably. Without *Ijtihad* the Muslim law would have remained stagnant and in irretrievable ruin. *Ijtihad* is similar in its functions to " the jus ediciendi " of the Roman magistrates Those persons who are entitled to resort to *Ijtihad* are known as Mujtahids and the Fatawas which they issue are similar to the "Responas" of the Roman jurists.

III

THE ADMINISTRATION OF JUSTICE BY THE KHULAFA-UR-RASHIDUN.

First Khalifa.

On the death of the Holy Prophet, Abu Bakr was elected as the first Khalifa of Islam, and during the brief era (about two years) of his administration, besides the Koran and the traditions which were the supreme laws of the land, the rule of *Ijma* was applied. In fact his own election was based on the broad principle of *Ijma.*

Abu Bakr administered justice according to the Koran and Hadis, and if any important issue presented to him, for which there was no precedent, then he used to decide it by *Ijma*, the consensus of opinion of the great followers of the Prophet Abu Bakr also resorted to *Ijtihad*, and Shah Wali Ullah calls him the founder of the doctrine of *Ijtihad* [1].

Umar who was the Chief Councillor was appointed as Kazi, the author of Sirat-us-Siddiiq asserts that people were so contented and honest that not a single case was filed in the Court of Umar [2]. However, the author of Shera Majmael bahriyn mention a case in which Umar himself was involved, and Khalifa Abu Bakr decided an important point of law, as to the custody of infants [3].

In the case of the upbringing of children the mother is preferred to the father and the following precedent is cited that 'Umar and his divorced wife approached Khalif Abu Bakr to decide this point. Abu Bakr

كتاب الطلاق.

شرح مجمع البحرين

وتقدم الام علي الاب فى الحضانة لما روي

ان عمر رضي الله عنه طلق زوجته فتنازعا الى

---

1 وہ رضی اللہ عنہ شیخ و استاد جمیع مجتہدین شد ازالۃ الخفا عن خلافۃ الخلفاء ۔

Izalatul-Khifa and Khilafatil-Khulafa.

2 ''قاضی حضرت عمر تھے اُس عہد کی صفائی معاملات کا یہ عالم تھا کہ ایک سال تک ایک مدعی بھی حضرت عمر کے سامنے نہ آیا'' – Sirat-us-Siddiq M. Habib-ur-Rahman Khan p. 103.

اس زمانہ کی صفائی معاملات کا یہ حال تھا کہ ایک سال تک کسی معاملہ میں کسی سے کوئی جھگڑا نہ ہوا ۔ اور کوئی مقدمہ حضرت عمر کی اجلاس میں نہیں آیا ۔ Muhammed Shah Khan Hayat-i-Siddiq Akbar p. 730.

3 According to the Hanafi law mother is to have the custody of male child till he reaches 7 years and female till puberty in preference to the father.

said "Oh Umar for this infant his mother's spit is better than honey which you may procure."

ابی بکر رضی الله عنه فقال ریقها خیر له من عسل عندک یا عمر -

Abu Bakr laid down another important law in the following case. "A man went to Abu Bakr and said 'My father desireth to take my property saying that he is in need of the whole of it' and bu Bakr said to his father; 'Surely that only of his property is thine which is sufficient for thy sustenance'; he answered " O Vicegerent of the Apostle of God, did not the Apostle of God say, 'thou and thy goods belong to thy father'. He replied, "Yes, but he meant by that only necessary maintenance."

In the law of inheritance the decision of Abu Bakr whether the grandfather excludes full brothers or sisters from inheritance served as a precedent, and the great Imam Abu Hanifa upheld it, and that has ever since been the rule of law for the Sunni Muslims of the Hanafi sect. The authorities for and against the right of grandfather to exclude brother and sisters are as follows:

For
1. Abu Bakr
2. Imam Abu Hanifa.

Against
1. Abu Yusuf } the chief disciples of Imam Abu Hanifa.
2. Muhammad }
3. Imam Malik.
4. Imam Shafii.
5. Ali the fourth Khalifa.
6. Zayd.

It may be noticed here that the Shia, the Shafii and the Maliki follow the opposite view to the Hanafi Sunni [2].

---

1. Jarrett. H. S. History of the Caliphs by Jalaluddin As-Sayuti (Bibliothica Indica) P. 100.
2. The division will be thus taking a simple case.

	According to Abu Bakr and Abu Hanifa	According to Ali.	According to Zaid.
Grandmother	1·6	1·6	1·6
Grandfather	5·6	1·6	Joint share 5·6
Sister	excluded	1-2	
Consanguine sister	excluded	1·6	

The second Khalifa.

In A. D.634 Umar succeeded Abu Bakr and his accession to office marks the beginning of an important era in the history of Islam. The boundaries of the Muslim Empire were extended far and wide and the administration of justice and law, and the maintenance of peace and order was perfect The judiciary was quite separate from the executive. It is interesting to read the famous firmans sent by Umar to Abu Musa Ashari, the Governor of Kufa and to Kazi Shurayh.

After the praise to God the administration of Justice is a duty. The Court must observe equality between the parties so that the weaker party may expect justice and the stronger may not expect concession. The burden of proof is on the plaintiff and the defendant may be put on oath, but let this not defeat the end of justice and law. If you have decided a case, then after due care and thinking you may revise your decision. If you are doubtful in a point which is mentioned in the Koran and Hadis then think over it again and again and then apply "Qiyas" (a procsss of deduction). When a party wants to tender evidence then fix a time limit and if he proves his case then decide accordingly. All Muslims are fit to be witnesses except those who have received the prescribed punishment

شريح

اما بعد فان القضاء فريضة محكمة و سنة
متبعة فآس بين الناس في وجهك و مجلسك
و عدلك ولا يطمع الشريف في حيفك البينة على
من ادعى واليمين على من انكر الصلح جائز الا
صلحاً احل حراما او حرم حلالا ولا يمنعك قضاء
قضيته بالامس فراجعت فيه نفسك ان ترجع
الى الحق الفهم الفهم فيما يتلجلج في صدرك
مما لم يبلغك في الكتاب والسنة واعرف الامثال
و الاشباه ثم قس الامور عند ذلك و اجعل لمن
ادعى بينة امداً ينتهي اليه فان احضر بينة
اخذت له بحقه و الا وجهت القضاء عليه
والمسلمون عدول بعضهم على بعض الا مجلوداً
في حد ومجربا في شهادة زور او ظنينا في ولاء
او قرابة -

(flogging) for hadd (fornication, adultery) and those who have tendered false evidence.

Here is the text of the firman sent to Kazi Shurayh.

"It is related by Shurayh that 'Umar wrote to him, that if a case is presented to him which is treated in the Koran then decide accordingly, and don't go against the Koranic injunctions, and if such a case is presented to him which is not treated in the Koran, then follow it in the Hadis and decide accordingly, but if a case is presented to him about which there is no provision in the Koran and Hadis, then look for its solution in the Ijma ul' Umat and follow that decision. However if such a case is presented to you about which there is no precedent in the Koran and Hadis, and not even decided by anyone before you then you may decide it according to your own judgment after due care and caution. I approve of such a course"

دارمی

عن شريح ان عمر بن الخطاب كتب اليه
ان جاءك شيء في كتاب الله فاقض به ولا يلفتك
عنه الرجال فان جاءك ما ليس في كتاب الله
فانظر سنة رسول الله صلى الله عليه وسلم
فاقض بها فان جاءك ما ليس في كتاب الله
ولم يكن فيه سنة من رسول الله صلى الله
عليه وسلم فانظر ما اجتمع عليه الناس فخذ
به فان جاءك ما ليس في كتاب الله ولم يكن
في سنة رسول الله صلى الله عليه وسلم ولم
يتكلم فيه احد قبلك فاختر اي الامرين شئت ان
شئت ان تجتهد برأيك ثم تقدم فتقدم وان
شئت ان تتأخر فتأخر ولا ارى التأخر الا خيرا
لك -

From the above firmans we can deduce the following important conclusions. That as early as the reign of 'Umar the Muslim law had accepted the view, (1) that the burden of proof is generally on the plaintiff, (2) that the judge may rely on his private judgment provided the decision is not against the provision of law, (3) and that the Judge may review his own judgment.

Umar like Abu Bakr used to decide all points on which there was no precedent by Ijma by debating on the point in the assembly of the Ashab of the Prophet , and 'Umar like Abu Bakr also resorted to Ijtihad There is a case reported in which 'Umar went against an Hadis. According to the Muhammadan Law a divorced woman by Tilaq-i-bain is entitled to residence and maintenance during the period of *iddat*. The Koranic injunction was اسکنوهن من حیث سکنتم which means that a divorced woman is entitled to the house. In a case it was argued before Umar that according to this provision of the Koran a divorced woman is not entitled to maintenance and Fatima b nt Qays deposed that when she was divorced, she enquired from the Prophet whether she had a right to residence and maintenance or not. The Prophet answerd in the negative. 'Umar on hearing this Hadis retorted that he would not give up the plain Koranic injunction as against this report and that it was possible that the woman had not remembered the Hadis correctly. The Shafii apparently follows this Hadis. They allow no maintenance to the woman irreversibly divorced unless she be pregnant.

Similarly in another case 'Umar created a precedent in accepting the evidence of an expert, A defamatory suit was filed in his court by Zibriqan bin Badr against a poet Hutaya alleging that a verse composed by the poet was defamatory It was not quite clear from the verse in dispute whether it was defamatory or not. So 'Umar summoned the poet Hassan bin Sabit and decided the case according to the expert's opinion [2].

Once 'Umar purchased a horse on approval and he allowed a rider to test it. The horse was injured in the course of the trial. Umar wanted to return the horse, and the owner refused to take it back. Eventually this case was referred for decision

---

1. Shah Wali-ullah mentions this in Hujjat-ul-baligha and says that 'Umar's fatwas were circulated all over the Muslim World.

2. Maulana Shibli's Alfaruq. p. 60.

to Shurayh who observed, "that if the horse was used for the purpose of riding with the permission of the owner then it could be returned otherwise not." It is said that Umar was pleased with the judgment and appointed Shurayh Kazi at Kufa.

Umar had once a law suit against a Jew and both of them went to the Kazi who on seeing the Imam rose in his seat out of deference. 'Umar considered this such an unpardonable weakness on the part of the Kazi that he dismissed him at once"[1]. Once Umar found his son Abu Shama drunk and he had him publicly flogged.

Umar was the first to allow suitable allowances to the persons holding the post of Kazis, for instance, Kazi Shurayh and Sulayman Rabia were paid five hundred dirhams per month, and all Kazis were prohibited from taking part in any business.

Umar appointed such judicious and capable persons as Kazis that they were universally respected throughout the Muslim world. Zayd bin Sabit was appointed to administer justice in Medina. He is well known as writer of the Koran in the time of the Holy Prophet. Kab bin Sur al-Azdi a judicious and critical lawyer was appointed Kazi at Basra. Abbadah bin as-samit was posted at Falastin. He had learnt the Koran by heart, and ranked among the first five Hafizs in the time of the Prophet. The great jurist Abdullah bin Masud was appointed Kazi at Kufa. He is the real founder of the Hanafi School of Jurisprudence. The other great Kazis were the eminent jurists Shurayh, Jamil bin Mamar, al-Jumahi, Abu Maryam al-hanafi, Sulayman bin Rabia, Albahili, Abdur Rahman bin Rabia, Abu qurrat ul-kindi and Imran bin al-Hasayn.[2]

Criminal Courts.

'Umar did not create criminal courts as distinct from civil courts. generally all important crimes such as murder, theft, and adultery were tried by the same courts ; however the initiative was always taken by the department of police which is technically known as Ahdas, and the

1. Abdur Rahim, Jurisprudence P.21.

2. The prescribed punishment by Shera is 80 stripes.

officer in charge was known as Sahib-ul-Ahdas. There were no jails before the reign of Umar. He was the first to assign a building as public jail in Mecca,[1] and thereafter jails were built in other places. The introduction of the jail system resulted in substituting many of the harsh punishments provided in Islam into confinement to Jails for instance Abu Mahjan Saqfi who was a great drunkard was sent to Jail instead of receiving the prescribed punishment of Hadd. 'Umar also introduced the sentence of transportation, for instance, the same person was transported to a definite place.[2]

Fadak.

The case of Fadak has been the subject of much misrepresentation by various sects of Islam. The decision of Abu Bakr and thereafter of 'Umar to treat Fadak as State property has established one of the most important constitutional precedents that the Khalifa in the capacity of ruler owns no private property. The facts of the case are as follows Immediately after the battle of Khaybar, Yusha bin Nun the head of the people of Fadak, on the mission of Mahiza bin Masud of his own accord peacefully surrendered Fadak to the Prophet of Islam, since then the income of this property was used by the Prophet partly for his personal expenses and also for the poor. On the death of the Prophet, his daughter Fatima claimed that she inherited Fadak from her father. This contention was overruled by Abu Bakr mainly on the ground of the following Koranic verse found in Sura Hashr.

The land or property which has been acquired, belongs to God, His Apostle, the orphans, the needy, the way-farer, ..the poor and the Muhajirin.. and all those who will come in future.

The Koran,
Part XXVIII Ch. LIX.

ما افاء الله على رسوله من اهل القرى فلله
و للرسول ولذى القربى واليتامى والمساكين وابن
السبيل... الله والمهاجرين الذين أخرجوا من
ديارهم... والذين جاءو من بعدهم -

---

1. Umar purchased the house of Safwan bin' Ummiyyah at Mecca for four thousands dirhems and turned it into Jail.

2. Maulana Shibli's Alfaruq p. 162.

Hence the land acquired by conquest or peaceful means by the head of the State is the waqf property for the benefit of all Muslims. Against this theory there is a traditional custom of the Arabs to divide the property between the warriors, and it is then inherited by their heirs The Prophet himself observed this custom when he distributed Khaybar to all his followers, but thereafter the Prophet did not distribute any other part of the country which he annexed or conquered. Accordingly Abu Bakr held Fadak to be the State property, or the State property set apart for the use of the Khalifa in accordance with the practice of the Prophet. It was in this capacity that the fourth Khalif Ali and thereafter his eldest son Hasan succeeded to the property of Fadak. On the death of Abu Bakr, Ali and Abbas made another representation to 'Umar to annul the decision of Abu Bakr. 'Umar in confirming the decision of the first Khalif pointed out that this rule will apply to all countries annexed by conquest or otherwise, and Fadak could not be made an exception to the rule.[1] However the Umayyad Khalifa Umar II restored Fadak to the Prophet's descendants.

Historically the origin of the Muslim law of Waqf is traced to a dedication made by Umar. It is related in the Tirmizi that Umar, had acquired a piece of land in Khaybar, and he sought Prophet's advice to make the pious use of it, thereupon

---

1. The view of 'Umar is reported in Bukhari thus.

"The Prophet while he was alive used to draw money (from Fadak) for his annual expenses and the rest he used to spend as the property of God. One his death Abu Bakr obtained possession of it as the Prophet's successor and maintained the same practice. On his death I (Umar) am his successor and it has been in my possession for the last two years and I have maintained the practice set forth by the Prophet of God."

صحیح بخاری

فكان رسول الله ينفق على اهله نفقة سنتهم
من هذا المال ثم يأخذ ما بقي فيجعله مجعل
مال الله فعمل رسول الله بذلك حياته ثم توفى
الله نبيه صلى الله عليه وسلم فقال ابوبكر انا
ولى رسول الله ثم توفى الله ابابكر فكنت انا
ولى ابى بكر فقبضتها سنتين من امارتي
اعمل فيها بما عمل رسول الله صلى الله عليه
وسلم و بما عمل فيها ابوبكر -

2. Sheikh Mazharul-Haq Sawanih Umri. Umar bin Abdul Aziz in) Urdu) p. 110.

the Prophet said "Tie up the property (asl., corpus) and devote the usufruct to human beings, and it is not to be sold or made the subject of gift or inheritance, devote its produce to your children, your kindred and the poor in the way of God.[1]" However Shibli observes that the first Waqf of Islam was made when the Prophet laid the foundation of the mosque of Medina [2]

Third Khalifa.

The Khalifa Usman was a pious and holy man, he maintained the judicial reforms initiated by Umar. He was succeeded by Ali.

Fourth Khalifa.

Ali was a great jurist and the most learned of the lawyers in the law of inheritance. Khalifa Umar said frequently that "Ali is the best of us in judicial decisions" and it is reported by Ibn A'bbas that Umar once declared "whenever a trustworthy person tells me a judgment of Ali I do not deviate from it" Aysha said of Ali, "Verily he is the most learned in the Sunnat". Ali like his predecessors upheld Ijma and also resorted to Ijtihad. In the Law of Inheritance Ali was the founder of "the doctrine of the Increase, Awl" The case is commonly known as *mimberiyya*, because it was answered by Ali when he was in the pulpit. The case was as follows :—

A Muslim died leaving a wife, two daughters and both his parents. The original Koranic shares are.—

Parent's each	$\frac{1}{6}$	=	$\frac{4}{27}$ $\frac{4}{27}$	} after abatement.
Wife	$\frac{1}{8}$	=	$\frac{3}{2}$	
Daughters	$\frac{2}{3}$	=	$\frac{16}{27}$	

The sum total of the fractions $\frac{27}{24}$ thus exceeded unity. The decision of Ali was that the shares must abate rateably. It is followed by the Sunni Muslims, but the Shia jurist hold that in such a contingency the share of the daughter alone must be decreased so as to reduce the sum-total of the fractions to unity[3].

1. Ameer Ali Mahommedan Law, Vol. 1, p. 152.
2. Siratun-Nabi, Vol. 1, p. 241.
3. Thus according to Shia law in the above example the collective shares of the daughters shall be 13-24 only.

Here is an interesting narrative—a case decided by Ali.

" Two men were sitting down, eating their morning meal, and one of the two had five loaves, and the other three loaves, and when they had placed the meal before them, a man passed and saluted them and they said 'sit down and eat,' and he sat down and eat with them, and they shared equally in their meal, the eight loaves, and the man arose and threw to them eight dirhams and said, "take these in exchange for what I have eaten belonging to ye two and have received of your food." They then quarrelled over it and the owner of the five loaves said, "for me are five dirhams and for thee three" and the owner of the three loaves exclaimed, 'I shall not agree unless the dirhams are divided equally between us,' and they took their case before Ali, the prince of the Faithful and related to him their adventure, and he said to the owner of the three, ' Verily thy companion hath offered to thee what he hath offered, and his loaves were more than thine, therefore be content with three ' But he replied, 'By Allah, I will not be satisfied with him except in my exact due.' And Ali said, 'in bare right thou shouldst have only one dirham and he seven dirhams.' And the man said, 'Good God! ' and Ali answerd 'that is so' The other said, 'Inform me of the grounds of this being my bare right, that I may acquiesce in it ' Ali answered, 'Are there not in eight loaves, four and twenty thirds which ye have eaten and ye are three men ? and it is not known who is the greatest eater amongst ye and who the least, you will therefore be considered in your eating as equal.' He went on, 'now thou hast eaten eight-thirds, and verily thou hadst but nine-thirds, and thy companion eat eight-thirds, and he owned fifteen-thirds of which he eat eight –there remain of his, therefore, seven which the owner of the dirhams eat, and he eat of what belonged to thee one out of nine. Therefore for thee is one for thy one, and for him seven. And the man exclaimed "Now I am content." [1]

1. Jarrett H. S. History of the Caliphs by Jalal Uddin A's-Sayuti. (Bibliotheca Indica) p. 183.

Another well known case which was decided by Kazi Shurayh between the Khalifa Ali and a Jew is as follows :—

Ali lost a coat of mail belonging to him on his way to Siffin, after the termination of the war Ali returned to Kufa, and there he saw his armour in the hands of a Jew and he said to the Jew. "This armour is mine," I neither sold it nor gave it away." The Jew answered, "It is my armour and in my possession.' "They both went to the court of Shurayh. "Shurayh said 'Proceed O prince of the Faithful' and he said, 'yes - this armour which is in the hand of this Jew is my armour —I neither sold it nor gave it away.' Shurayh exclaimed 'What dost thou say, O Jew ?' He replied, 'it is my armour and in my possession.' Then Shurayh said, 'hast thou any proof, O prince of the Faithful ?' He said, 'yes, Kambar and al-Hasan are witnesses that the armour is my armour.' Shurayh replied 'the evidence of a son is not admissible in favour of a father !" The judgment was given in favour of the Jew. At this the Jew exclaimed, "I testify that there is no God but God, and I testify that Muhammad is the apostle of God and that this armour is thy armour."[1]

With the assasination of Ali the republican period of Islam ended The respect for law and order was the governing spirit of that age. The decisions of the Khulafa-ur rashidun were universally respected throughout the Muslim world. In this era the Muslim law was developed by the State, the bench and the bar, later on its development was confined to the works and opinions of the great jurists.

---

1. Jarrett H. S. History of the Caliphs by Jalal Uddin A's-Sayuti (Bibliotheca Indica) p. 188.

III

THE ADMINISTRATION OF JUSTICE DURING THE UMAYYAD KHILAFAT

Political history.

Muawiyah was appointed Governor of Syria by the second Khalifa Umar. He consolidated his power during the reign of Usman, and asserted his own right to the vacant khilafat as against 'Ali the fourth Khalifa. This led to the first Civil war of Islam. His reign was extremely unpopular in the beginning; however he was undoubtedly a capable and energetic Sovereign. Von Kremer observed, that "a strong personality like Muawiyah was necessary, and doubly necessary, to pacify the commotions of the time".[1] It is difficult to understand the succession of Yazid. How Muawiyah conversant with the follies of his son could have appointed him as his successor is one of the anomalies which history presents.[2]

Muawiyah died in A. D. 680. He was succeeded by his son Yazid whose reign is sullied by three acts which have never been forgiven by the Muslims— (1) The tragedy of Kerbala, the brutal murder of Husayn, (2) the pillage of Medina, (3) the siege of Mecca. Another Umayyad King 'Abdul Malik found himself in a critical position,[3] and with

---

1. S. Khuda Bukhsh. History of Islamic Civilization, p. 221.

2. Ibn Qutaybah refers to a letter of Husayan sent to Muawiyah. It runs thus "......I have never intended to fight with you...... although I fear that God will hold me responsible for leaving you alone and your unjust party......By God! Muawiyah you behave in a manner that would lead people to think that you are not one of the Muslims and they have no part or lot with you......Verily I know nothing that safeguards better my interest and the interest of my religion and the followers of Muhammed than waging holy war against you......Fear God, O Muawiyah......God will never forgive your killing men......and your appointing as your successor a youth who drinks wine and hunts with dogs." S. Khuda Bukhsh, History of Islamic civilization Introduction, p. 22.

3. At this period there were three rival claimants to the khilafat. Abdullah ibu Zubayr was at Mecca, Muhammad Ibnul Hanafiyyah was supported by Mukhtar. The Kharijite leader was Najdina-ibn-Amir.

difficulty, he consolidated his empire. A notable exception was Umar Ibn ' Abdul Aziz. He was a son of a grand-daughter of Khalifa Umar. He is regarded by the Sunni Muslims as the pious Khalifa (Al-Khilafat-us-Saleh) and as the fifth of the Khulafa-ur-rashidun. He was a great lawyer and a notable theologian; during his reign the Muslim jurisprudence was greatly developed. Merwan II was the last of the Umayyad Kings.

Justice.

The administration of Justice was carried out by the Kazis appointed by the Umayyad Kings. According to Mawardi the appointment or the dismissal of the Kazi had to be publicly announced.[1]

Similar to Wizarat there were Kazis with limited and unlimited powers. A Kazi with limited judicial powers was restricted to duties specified in the firman of appointment. The Kazi with unlimited powers had an extensive jurisdiction, and exercised complete supervision on all things authorised by the law. The important executive duties were :—

(1) The appointment of guardians.

(2) The administration of Waqf properties.

(3) Execution of punishment as prescribed by the law.

(4) Looking after testamentary dispositons.

(5) Supervision of subordinate Kazis, and other law officers notaries, *shohud* and secretaries, *umana*.

(6) To lead the Friday prayers.

There was no regular court of appeal, but the board for the inspection of grievances; the Nazir-ul-Mazalim, effectually controlled the judiciary. Its function was to set right cases of miscarriage of justice. It is stated that on the analogy of the Khulafa-ur-rashidun who

1. When the Kazi died all his subordinate staff forfeited their posts and if necessary had to be re-appointed.

used to hear complaints and decide cases, the Umayyad Khalifa 'Abdul-Malik inaugurated this board and he himself heard appeals. He used to refer intricate law points to the famous Kazi, 'Abu Idris Auzi. After him 'Umar ibn 'Abdul 'Aziz was particular in personally receiving complaints and hearing appeals. The later Umayyad Khalifas also followed this practice. Von Kremer observes that on the analogy of this institution a similar board was established by King Roger the Norman ruler of Sicily.

IV

THE ADMINISTRATION OF JUSTICE OF MUSLIM LAW IN SPAIN

Political history.

The Khalifas of Damascus possessed an extensive Empire, it extended beyond the Oxus and the Pyrenees, on the shores of the Caspian and in the fertile valley of the Nile. In A. D. 711 the famous Muslim general Tariq ibn Ziyad defeated the Visigoths under Roderic. The Umayyad Khalifas continued to exercise suzerainty over Spain for a long time. After the overthrow of the Umayyad dynasty by the Abbaside, a Umayyad prince 'Abdur-Rahman escaped and fled to Africa, he eventually reached Spain, and in A. D. 756 established the Umayyad dynasty of Spain. Till the advent of Abdur-Rahman I, the Khutba in the mosque was read in the name of the Abbaside Khalifa 'Abu Jafar-Al-Mansur, but 'Abdur Rahman after ten years reign ordered Khutba to be read in his own name.[1] Abdur Rahman 'Ansari was the first to style himself Khalifa and Amir-ul-Muminin. The Muslim Khilafat of Spain continued till the deposition of Hisham III in A. D. 1031[2]. The Khilafat was succeeded by the Council of State under Ibn Jahwar as the first Consul. The Muslim power ruled in Spain till A. D. 1538, and they were driven out from Andalusia in A. D. 1610.

Law and Justice.

Before the death of Hisham A. D. 796, the Fakihs of Spain had come into prominence. These jurists belonged to the Maliki School of jurisprudence. The Abbaside Khalifas were inimical to Imam Malik because of his alleged support to a pretender

1. Nawab. Zulkader Jung Bahadur Khilafat Andalusia (Urdu) p. 22.

2. Hisham III was publicly deposed in the mosque by the waziers notables and Sheikhs. they declaring that henceforth the council of State has assumed the reins of government.

and he is said to have declared that "in Hisham he saw the ideal of a Muslim King and he proclaimed him alone worthy of sitting on the Khalifa's throne."[1] Accordingly Imam Malik's disciples were welcomed in Spain, and in fact Hisham appointed the judges and ecclesiastics from this Sunni School. Yahya ibn Yahya was the most renowned pupil of Imam Malik. It is related that Imam Malik called him the 'Aqil (subtle, sagacious and learned man,) of Spain. Yahya was greatly revered at Cordova. Another great Maliki jurist was Talha.[2] The Maliki jurisprudence ever since exercised great influence in the Muslim Spain. During the reign of the Almoravides the theologians and Fakihs were very powerful [3].

The Muslims of Spain had imported the same system of administration of justice as was prevalent in Medina and Damascus. The chief Kazi aided by subordinate Judges administered justice according to the Koranic law. The Court of Justice was usually near the city mosques and frequently the mosques were used as the local Courts. During the reign of 'Abdur-rahman I there were four Chief Kazis, Kazi-ul-Kzat in Spain[4]. They are also known as Kazi-ul-Jamat. In small towns the Judge appointed was known as *musaddid*[5]. Closely associated with the duties of Kazi and under his supervision was the Sahib-ul-Madina commonly known as Sahib-ul-lail who was responsible for the execution of the sentence of death or of Hudd, the prescribed punishment for whoredom and intoxication, etc. The sentence of death

---

1. R. Dozy Spanish Islam, p. 243.

2. The Maliki jurists including Yahya and Talha had raised a rebellion against Hakam. However the Sultan pardoned all the Fakihs.

3. The Maliki jurists were so orthodox that they had interdicted on pain of death and confiscation of entire property, the celebrated book of Imam Ghazali the Revival of Religious science.

4. Syed Muhammed Khan. History of Spain (in Urdu) p. 418.

5. Nafhut-Tib of al-Maqqari. Tr. by M. Khalilur-Rahman (in Urdu) p. 49.

was executed after it was confirmed by the Khalifa. The Muhtasib was responsible for maintaining fixed standard for the purchase and sale of all commodities.

The traditional custom of the Khalifas to hear cases in person was in existence in Spain, but it was not so common as at Damascus. Amir Hisham-ar-razi is credited with hearing such suits[1]. Apparently this Court and the Court of the waziers known as the Council of State, where state trials were held was the Supreme Court of the State. The Court of the Kazi-ul-Kuzat was the Chief Appellate Court where appeals from the subordinate Courts were filed. There were Muftis also who generally advised the Kazis in interpreting and applying the law[2].

One of the most learned jurists was Ibn Bashir who acted during the reign of Hakam as the Chief Kazi of Spain. His judgments were respected throughout the Muslim world. It is related that al-Hakam's uncle Said al-Khayr had a case pending before Ibn Bashir. It was required to prove the disputed deed by the evidence of marginal witnesses. One of the witnesses happened to be Hakam himself. The monarch's presence was thus indispensable and he was accord ingly summoned to appear in the Court[3]. On another occasion Ibn Bashir decreed a suit against al-Hakam, and ordered the monarch to deliver possession of the disputed land to the plaintiff. It is related that al-Hakam sent for the plaintiff and purchased the land from him[4].

Ibn Ali 'Amir styled Almansur was one of the greatest

---

1. Nafhut-Tib by al-Maqqari tr. by M. Khalilur-Rahman. (Urdu) p. 254.

2. Yahya ibn Ziyad, Abu Umer, Abdul-Malik bin Habib Sulami, Abu' Ibrahim, 'Abu 'Abdullah al-Husayn Kazi Abu Hafiz bin Umar Kazi-Munzir bin Said, 'Umar, ibn Bashir, Bashir ibn Qatan, 'Abdullah ibn Musa and Hamid ibn Muhammad were the famous jurists and Kazis of Spain.

3. Nawab Zukader Jung Bahadur Khilafat-i-Andalvsia (in Urdu) p. 44.

4 Ibid, p. 41.

Prime Ministers (Hajib) of Spain; in fact he was sovereign de facto. His love of justice and equity was proverbial. He was for sometime Chief Justice at Mauritania. It is related that a man presented himself in the wazier's Court, and accused the shield-bearer of al-Mansur of breach of contract, and of refusing to appear in the court of the Kazi to answer the charge. He reported that the judge also had not compelled the shield-bearer to present himself in the Court. Thereupon al-Mansur became indignant and ordered the prefect of the police to conduct these two men to the Court of the Kazi. 'Abdur-rahman ibn Futais, the judge, having decided the case in favour of the plaintiff, he appeared to thank the minister. "Spare me thy thanks, said the minister " thou has gained thy case, "[1]. On another occasion an African merchant approached Al-Mansur and accused his major-domo who thinking that he was shielded from legal proceedings in virtue of his high office had declined to appear in the Court of the Kazi. The Minister instantly placed the major-domo under arrest, and sent him to the Court, and on hearing that the case was decided in favour of the African merchant he deprived his major-domo of office.[2]

The idea of State trials for nobility was known to the Muslims of Spain. We have a complete account of the trial of Mushay who was sometime private secretary to Hakam, Governor of Majorca and lastly Secretary of state. He was tried by the Council of State composed of several Waziers notably Ibn Jabir, Ibn Jahwar and Ibn Iyash. His property was declared sequestrated and he was imprisoned in the state prison at Al-zahra.

There was another notable state trial of 'Abdul-Malik Ibn Mundhir, President of the Court of Appeal and the poet

1. R. Dozy Spanish Islam, p. 532.
2. R. Dozy Spanish Islam, p. 485.

Ramadī for high treason. The eunuch Jaudhar was selected by the conspirators for the young Khalifas' assassination their object was to put on throne Abdur-rahman Ibn Obaidullah. The conspiracy failed and the conspirators were brought to trial before the Councl of State. The decision was based on the verse of the Koran (Sura. V.) " Behold the recompense of those who war against God and His Messenger and go about to commit disorders on the earth, shall be that they shall be slain or crucified, or have their alternate hands and feet cut off or be banished the land "[1]. The pretender and the president of the Court of Appeal were sentenced to death, Jaudhar was crucified, the poet Ramadi was not banished but allowed to remain in Cordova under strict supervision. It is stated that later on he was pardoned.

The Muslim law is very strict in punishing people who blasphemed the Prophet of Islam and their religion. Such instances were common in Spain. The self-styled martyrs sought glorification cheaply; to achieve that end they had merely to revile the Prophet. The Monk Isaac was the first to set the example. He was condemned to death by the Kazi of Cordova. The trial of the famous monk Evlogius had caused a sensation. He was also condemned to death.[2] Similarly Leocritia a Muslim girl on apostasy was convicted and sentenced to death.[3]

---

1. R. Dozy Spanish Imam, p. 489.

2. The others who were condemned to death for blasphemy were Sancho, Jeremias, Habentius and Paul.

The Christians were apparently not in sympathy with these martyrs. they said (R. Dozy Spanish Islam, p. 286). "The Sultan allows us to exercise our own religion and does not oppress us; to what purpose, then, is this fanatical Zeal? Those whom you dub martyrs are nothing of the kind: they are suicides. . . ."

3. It is said that Leocritia was beheaded and thrown into the river, and there is a story that she was buried in the church of S. Genet. A. B. C. Dunbar, Dict. of Saintly women (1904) i. p. 468.

V

THE ADMINISTRATION OF JUSTICE DURING THE ABBASIDE KHILAFAT

Political history.

The first Abbaside ruler was known as al-Saffah. At his death in A. D. 754 he nominated Abu Jafar his brother as his successor. Abu Jafar is the real founder of the dynasty. The first nine Sovereigns of the house of Abbas were men of extraordinary ability—all devoted to the welfare of their subjects. The reign of Harun is noteworthy for the expansion of the Hanafi System of jurisprudence. Abu Yusuf the chief disciple of Imam Abu Hanifa was the Chief Justice, Kazi-ul-Kuzat at that time. During the reign of the Abbaside monarchs the Persian influence played an important role in external as well as the internal history of Islam. Dr. Nicholson holds, that "the Revolution which enthroned the Abbasides marks the beginning of a Moslem as opposed to an Arabian Empire."[1] In A. D. 1258, the Abbaside dynasty was thrown over by the great conqueror Hvlaku Khan. For two years there was no Khalifa in Islam. The Mameluke Sultan of Egypt,[2] Malik-al-Zahir Baybars revived the Khilafat in offering it to 'Ahmad' Abul-Qasim a scion of the Abbaside house. Henceforth it was merely a spiritual office.

Justice.

The administration of justice was carried on by the Kazis with limited and unlimited powers. Their functions were in general similar to those of the Kazis during the time of the Umayyad Khalifas. The institution of Nazir-ul-Mazalim was also in vogue. Of the Abbaside Khalifas notably Mahdi, Hadi, Harun and Mamun generally received complaints, and heard appeals to set right cases of miscarriage of justice. The last Khalifa who kept up this practice was Muhtadi. Later on

1. A literary history of the Arabs, p. 254.

2. This dynasty was founded in A. D. 1250 by Aybak a Turkish slave of the Ayyubid Malik Salih Najmul Din. It continued till A. D. 1517.

a special officer known as the president was appointed to hold and preside at sittings of the Nazir-ul-Mazalim[1]. A Wazir with unlimited powers could preside but a Wazir or Governor with limited powers had to be specially nominated as president by the Khalifa.

The position of the president was higher than that of the Kazi, the latter was under the supervision and control of the president. Mawardi maintains that the president was not bound by the strict letter of the law ; he could apply the principles of equity to secure the ends of justice. The president usually fixed a day to receive petitions. He could hear witnesses on either side, and he might refer the parties to an arbitrator.

Besides these the chief duties of the president were:

(1) To supervise and control Waqf properties.

(2) To execute judicial decisions which the Kazi was powerless to enforce.

(3) To maintain public order and protection of divine services and prayers.

(4) To supervise the officers in charge of chancery, and finance and taxes, and to investigate into the oppressive conduct of executive officers, and thereby initiate proceedings *ex-officio*.

The president s court consisted of Court ushers, Judges and men learned in law to solve difficult law questions, secretaries to record minutes of the work and recorders to carry out the directions of the Court[2]. It was in about A. D. 1176 that Nurudin Mahmud who was a great jurist and a traditionist established a High Court of Justice called *the Dar-ul-adl*, and he organised and greatly improved the judiciary[3].

---

1. It is said that under Muqtader the mistress of the robes was allowed to hold the sittings of this board surrounded by jurists on every Friday in the Mausolleum situated on the Rufsafah.

2. S. Khuda Bukhsh. The Orient under the Caliphs, p. 289.

3. Ameer Ali, a short History of Saracens, p. 341 and p. 423.

VI

THE ADMINISTRATION OF JUSTICE BY THE FATIMID KHALIFAS

North Africa.

The Berber States still flourished in North Africa, and the fugitive Muslims took refuge there. It is said that "North Africa was always the home of the lost causes of Islam." It was here that an Isma 'ilian[1] preacher Abdullah established his religion[2]. Here their leader Mahdi appeared and settled at Kairawan. In 301 A. H. (A. D. 912) the Mahdi founded the city of al Mahadiya near Kairawan and it served as the Fatimid capital for some generations. In A. D. 933 the Mahdi died he was succeeded by his son Abdul-Kasim-Al-Qaim the second Fatimid Khalifa. Al-Móizz, the fourth Fatimid Khalifa was determined to struggle for the conquest of Egypt, and ultimately his general Jawhar succeeded in annexing Egypt. Al-Móizz claimed descendant from the House of Ali. The greatest of the Fatimid Khalifa was Al-Hakim. The last of the Fatimid Khalifa was, All 'Adid. In A. D. 1168 the rule of the Abbaside Khalifas was established in Egypt by the renowned leader Salah-uddin who had also put an end to the Latin Kingdom of Jerusalem. The Fatimid Khilafat had its origin in a religious subsect of Islam, the Fatimid Khalifas claimed to be the legitimate Khalifas of all Muslims and not only rulers of Egypt. They considered the Abbaside as usurpers of their rights.

Justice.

The administration of justice was carried out by the Kazis in accordance with the laws of Islam, and similar to the Nazr-ul-Mazalim, during the reign of Al-Móizz, 'every Sunday a court was held for the inspection of complaints, and to hear petitions against officials. The court consisted of the *Kaid*, Military

1. The Ismailians are partisans of Ismail, son of Jafar as Sadiq, the sixth Imam.

Governor, the Wazir the Kazi, and other learned men in the law. This court did not try cases, it simply referred them to the proper Kazi with such orders as it deemed fit. The decision then came before the Court of inspection of complaints, and after being written out in full legal form by a secretary, it was submitted to the Khalifa for confirmation. This authoritative decision was communicated to the petitioner. The chief Kazi of Egypt had jurisdiction over all the territories subject to the Fatimid rule[1]. There is a very interesting narrative mentioned by Severus of Ashmunayn. A merchant filed a suit in the court of Kazi against the Khalifa Al-Hakim who was summoned to appear before the Kazi. On the Khalifa's appearance the Kazi treated him like an ordinary party in a case before him. The merchant claimed compensation to the extent of 1,000 pieces of gold for the fruits which were destroyed by the Government officials. Hakim in his defence stated that the fruits destroyed were intended to be used for preparing drinks forbidden by the Koran, but if the merchant would swear that the fruits were not intended for that purpose he would pay compensation in lieu of their destruction. The merchant took the oath, and was accordingly paid compensation in the court, and he gave a formal receipt to the Khalifa. Dr. O'leary further narrates that "He (the merchant) then demanded letters of protection from the Khalifa that he might not incur any retaliation for his suit and these were given."[2] When the case was concluded the Kazi who all this time had treated the parties equally saluted the Khalifa as his lawful master. It is said Hakim admired the Kazi's conduct.

---

1. De Lacy O'leary. History of the Fatimid Khalifate, p. 103.
The income of the chief Kazi was about 15,000 pieces of Gold. ibid, p. 174.

2. Ibid, p 166.

VII
THE ADMINISTRATION OF JUSTICE IN THE TURKISH EMPIRE

Political history.

The foundation of the Ottoman Empire was laid by Artughril in a small principality in Asia Minor near the Bithynian province of the Byzantine Emperors. This great Turkish adventurer had received this province as a gift from the Seljukan Turk 'Ala-uddin, the Sultan of Iconium. From 'Artughril's son Usman the nation of Osmanli (Ottoman) Turks takes its national appellation. In 1288 Usman succeeded Artughril and established the Ottoman dynasty. Amurath I extended the Ottoman kingdom and his son Bajazet I was the first to obtain from the Abbaside Khalifa (who was at this time in Egypt) the superior title of Sultan. Bajazet's reign is famous for the struggle with the great world conqueror Timur, in which the latter was victorious. Bajazet died in captivity. At his death the Ottoman Empire lay in irretrievable ruin; however its past glories were to some extent retrieved by Muhammad I and Amurath II. The greatest of the Ottoman Sultans is Muhammad II surnamed the conqueror of Constantinople. In A. D. 1517 Salim I overthrew the Mamluke dynasty and annexed Egypt and obtained in his favour renunciation of the dignity of Khilafat from Mutawakkil the last Abbaside Khalifa and took possession of the sacred insignia of that high office.[1] Henceforth the Ottoman Sultans were known as the Khalifas of Islam. In short the Ottoman dynasty after ruling for about seven hundred years came to an end in March 1924. The last of the Ottoman ruler Sultan Abdul

1. C. M. D. 'Ohsson in his work Tableau general de' Empire Othoman doubts the accuracy of this popular account. Dr. T. W. Arnold in his recent book the Caliphate appears to be of the same opinion, Ch. XII, p. 139 and treats this narrative as a fiction, in his opinion "the first occasion on which such a claim was put forward in a diplomatic document is in the Treaty of Kuchuk Kainargi in 1774," ibid, p. 165.

Majid was deposed by the National Assembly of Angora. The institution of Khilafat was accordingly abolished, and Turkey became a Republic with Mustapha Kamal Pasha as the First President.

Administration of justice.

It has been remarked that according to the Muslim theory, justice is administered in "God's name". This conception is not the basis of the Turkish administration of Justice. The Ottoman Sultan is admittedly the fountain of Justice, and he is styled the "shadow of God upon earth." There is no trace says Creasy "in Turkish history of any civil constitutional restraint upon the will of the ruling sovereign."[1] The Ottoman Sultans possessed absolute power of life or death and property of his subjects. The Sultan combined the legislative and executive power. However the Sultan of his own accord or because of fear of revolution does not openly disregard the restraints of the Sacred Law of Islam. His Imperial edicts are subordinate to the Koran and the traditions. The edicts pronounced by the Sultan on ecclesiastical or temporal problems not provided for by the Islamic Sacred Law is designated Kanunnamah (the code of canons). The edicts are issued in consultation with the Mufti, or on his sanction by a solemn declaration of Fatwa. The lofty gate of the Royal Tent—La Porta Sublima—denotes the seat of Government and the place where the Sultans administered justice. The administration of justice is carried out by the Ulema—the order of men learned in Law. This body was organised by Muhammad the conqueror by founding Madrissas to serve as a training ground for the judges of the state. The students who were qualified in these Madrissas received the title of "danis-hmend"—gifted with knowledge. These danis-hmend "were required to go through an elaborate course of study of the Law to be qualified as Ulema.

History of the Ottoman Turks, p. 152.

The Sheikh-ul-Islam (mufti) is the head of the Judiciary, and he is the supreme interpreter of the Koran and the traditions of the Prophet. He sits twice every week[1] at the Supreme Court of Justice, Arzodessi, and adminsters justice as an Appellate and also original Court. The three Kadi-ul-Askers are the next high judicial functionaries. One of them is the Supreme Judge for Turkey in Europe., the other of the Asiatic provinces and the third frequently known as "Istambul Effendi" sits in Stambul proper. The Kazi-ul-Askers sit as an appellate Court and revise the sentences of all the Judges of the Empire within their respective jurisdiction, and twice in the week attend the Supreme Court of the Sheikh-ul-Islam. The Kazis are appointed as Judges of the smaller towns and rural district[2]. The Mullas act as Judges in the chief cities[3]. The Mapshati or Naib of the Kazi refers all doubtful and intricate points to the Kazi for his decision, and when the Kazi himself is in doubt he refers the case to the Kazi-ul-Asker, whose dicision is binding on the subordinate judiciary. The Turkish judicial System maintained the old principle of Muslim theory that no Muslim can be judged by a non-Muslim.

The head of Ulema was the Mufti. He exercised extensive power. He was the authoritative expounder of the law, and the sole legal authority for issuing fatawas. Instances occurred in Turkish history where the Mufti caused the Sultans to restrain passing laws and even abandon his projects. It has been argued that this officer exercised effective constitutional check on the Sultans prerogative, a veto similar to the Roman tribunes or the polish nobles. There are instances on record of a distinguished Mufti

---

1. Richard Davey, the Sultan and his subjects, Vol. I, p. 66.

During the reign of Selim III the diwan of the grand Vazier formed a court of justice it consisted of the "Vazier, Kapitan Pacha, the two kadiaskers the Nischaudjis and deftendars," Sir. E. Creasy. Vol. II, p. 323.

2. Sir E. Creasy, History of Ottoman Turks, p. 173.

3. R. Davey. The Sultan and his subjects, Vol. I, p. 74.

"Djemali" and Salim I the first Ottoman Khalifa which go tc establish this theory. On one occasion Salim had condemned to death about 150 of the persons employed in his treasury. Djemali pleaded on their behalf thus "It is the duty of the Mufti to have a care for the weal of the Sultan of Islam in the life to come. I therefore ask of thee the lives of 150 men unrighteously sentenced by thee to death.'"[1] The Sultan gave way to the learned Mufti. Similarly it is said when Salim had made up his mind to extirpate the Christians, Djemali intervened and said that Koran prohibited compulsory conversion and enjoined toleration, and through his efforts the Greek patriarch was granted audience of the Sultan. On another occasion Djemali saved the lives of 400 merchants condemned to death because they were found to be trading in silk with Persia in disobedience to an Imperial edict. It is related that Sultan Sulaiman the magnificent asked a great Mufti, Sheikh Abu Saoud to issue a fatwa declaring that it is lawful to put to death all non-muslims, of conquered provinces, who refused to accept Islam. The Mufti declined to issue such a fatwa.

Sir George Larpent in his short chapter on "Turkish administration of justice"[2] gives a very coloured view of the judicary and in his opinion the Turkish judiciary is corrupt. He ridicules the whole system including the office of Mufti. He says, "In general, let the cause be right or wrong, Christians or Jews have no chance against Turks except by dint of money—happy if even that can save them."[3]

In conclusion as a relief Sir George Larpent cites two remarkable decisions one of which fell under his own observation. "A ship freighted at Alexandria by Turks to convey them

1. Sir. E. Creasy, the History of the Ottoman Turks, Vol. I, 247.

2. Turkey its history and progress Vol I it is curions that in the introduction, p. V he disapproves of Ubicinis "letters surerla Turquie and" says. "The only fault this author has is a bias in favour of the Turks which leads him to regard everything in the most brilliant colours."

3. Ibid. p. 277.

and their merchandise, consisting of rice and dates, to Constantinople met with a violent storm on the passage. The master told the freighters who were on board, that he could not save the ship nor their lives, except by throwing into the sea all the goods upon deck. They consented not only for themselves, but for other freighters who were at Constantinople. When the ship arrived there those who had been on board joined with the others to sue the master of the ship in order to recover the value of the goods he had thrown overboard. The Mullah of Galata, before whom he was summoned had the case fully represented to him and his depvty as usual had the promise of reward. . When the parties appeared and the witnesses were examined, the Mullah reflected a while, took down his book and gravely opening it told them the book declared that the master should pay the true value of those very goods "that is what the freighters could prove by witnesses. . . . . . . The freighters ran out of court to find witnesses but the judge. . . . without further hesitation signed a written decree in favour of the master."[1]

" The second case was before a young Cadi of Smyrna. A poor man claimed a house which a rich man had seized. The former produced his deeds and instrument to prove his right, but the latter had provided a number of witnesses and to support their evidence more effectually, he presented the Cadi with a bag containing five hundred ducats which the Cadi received. When it came to hearing . . the judge calmly drew from beneath his sofa the bag of 500 ducats. . . . . . saying. . . . . . 'you have been much mistaken in the suit'. . . . and decreed the house to the poor plaintiff."[2]

The Shera courts took cognizance of the following cases " in civil law, questions concerning marriage, alimony, education of children, liberty, slavery, inheritance, wills,

---

1. Turkey, its History and Progress, p. 281.

2. Ibid, p. 282.

absence, and disappearance; in criminal law suits concerning retaliation, the price of blood, the price of laming a limb, the price of causing an abortion, damages, for disfigurements, the division of the price of blood."[1] The Nizamiyah, secular courts took cognizance of commercial and penal cases.[2] The Diwan's court also tried capital cases of great officials and in case of conviction a *chaush* was directed to execute the sentence.[3]

During the reign of Muhammad II Khusru Pasha prepared a code based on the Hanafi Law. Sulaiman who is named the Legislator ordered Sheikh Ibrahim bin Muhammad Al Halabi of Alleppo to prepare another code which appeared in 1549. It was called the Multaka-ul-Abhar "the confluence of the Seas"[4] the Majmae Al-Anhar by Abdur-Rahman known as Shaikh Zada is a commentary on the Multaka. The edicts of the Sultan were collected by the Mufti Abu Saoud and called the kanunnamah of Sulaiman.[5] The Durral-Al Hukkam by Mulla Khusru is a commentary by the same author on the Ghurar at Ahkam. The Kanunnamah-i-Jaza was the Turkish penal code it was published in Constantinople in A. D. 1838. The later Criminal Code was based on the code of Mapallan. The famous Turkish fatawas are: The Kitab fial Fiqk al Kadusi by Hafiz Muhammad him Ahmad Al-kadusi, published in 1821. The Falawa-i-Abdur Rahim Effendi collected by the Mufti Abdur Rahim. It was printed in 1827. The Tuhfat-as-Sukuk by Nuaman Effendi was published in 1832.

---

1. A Heidborn Maunel de droit public et administratif de l'empire Ottoman. p. 255.

2. A. H. Lybyer. The Ottoman Empire in the time of Suleiman, p. 155.

3. Ibid, p. 221.

4. The Multaka is the basis of D'Ohssons' excellent work. Tableau General de l'empire Ottoman, 7 vols.

5. Von. Hammer Staatsverfassung, p. 396.

Turkish Legal Reforms

Since the inauguration of the Republican movement in Turkey the Grand National Assembly of Angora has been passing legislative enactments of supreme importance. The old order has completely been replaced by modern democratic ideas in all spheres of life. The Turkish judicial system has also been reformed. The Grand National Assembly has enacted a new penal code of 600 articles adopted from the Italian code,[1] a new civil code of eighteen hundred articles taken from Switzerland,[2] and is to pass shortly a new commercial code of 700 articles borrowed from Germany. The Minister of Justice Mahmud Essad Bey is the eminent figure responsible for introducing these legal reforms. A new Faculty of Law has been constituted at Angora. It shall be the recruiting ground for the jurists and judges.

Since the abolition of the Capitulations the foreign powers were interested in the Turkish system of Administration of Justice, and undoubtedly they will welcome the new legal reforms. The old system has completely been replaced. There is at present a Supreme Court which sits at Eskishehr, but will be transferred to Angora on the completion of the new Law Court building. This Supreme Court consists of 32 members who are sub-divided in sections dealing with special cases. At the present moment there are about 600 subordinate tribunals who serve as the courts of first instance invested with civil and criminal jurisdiction. The appeals from these courts are filed in the Turkish Supreme Court. In short a new era has opened for Turkey, and it is not easy to realise the working of these judicial reforms or estimate its value at the present transient period.[3]

---

1. The Pioneer, Friday, March 5th, 1926.

2. The Pioneer, Sunday, Feb. 21st, 1926.

3. As regards marriage dower and divorce, the Muslim Law has been completely superseded. The Civil Code in accordance with the old law still prohibits the marriage of Muslim women with Christians.

EGYPT AS A TURKISH PROVINCE

Political status.

In A. D. 1517 Salim I conquered Egypt and since then land of Pharaohs ranked as an important part of the Turkish Empire. It continued nominally to be under the Ottoman Sultans till the declaration of the British Government on the eve of the Great War. At present Egypt is considered to be an independent State. The relation between the Ottoman Sultans and the Khedives of Egypt was laid down in various firmans dating from 1841 to 1892. The most important firman was granted to Tewfik Pasha in 1879. According to the firman of 1892 the civil and financial administration of Egypt is confided to the Khedive Abbas II and his male descendants in order of primogeniture. It was laid down in that firman that (1) all Egyptians are Ottoman subjects, (2) the taxes are levied in the Ottoman Sultan's name, (3) the Khedive had no right to make political treaties with foreign states.

Justice is administered in Egypt by the following Courts (1) the Mehkemeh Sheraieh, (2) the Native tribunals, (3) the Mixed tribunals and the Consular Courts.[1]

Tha Native tribunals established in 1883 administer justice between the Egyptians and also if an Egyptian commits a criminal offence against a European or another Egyptian he is tried by the Native tribunals. These tribunals administer justice according to the Egyptian (French) Code. However

1. The Mixed Court or the International Tribunals were created by Nubar Pasha at the instance of the great powers. The Court of Appeal sits at Alexandria and there are three Courts of first instance one at Cairo one at Alexandria and one at Mansourah. There are mixed European and Egyptian Judges. All the powers are represented on the Courts of first instance. The Mixed Court only exercise criminal jurisdiction over Europeans in certain specified cases. The Consular Courts usually try all cases in which foreigners are accused of committing crime according to the laws of his own country. The Mixed Courts try civil cause of dispute between the Egyptians and the Europeans.

all cases relating to marriage, inheritance, and will are tried in the Mehkemeh Sheraieh, by the Kazi who decides according to the Sheriat. In short the courts of Kazi deal with all questions affecting the personal status of the Muslims.

In Egypt there is also an order of the Ulema as prevalent in Turkey. The Mosque and the University of El-Azhar is the recruiting ground. The number of Ulema having the rank of "Alim" is limited. This rank carries with it the right to wear a special "pelisse." The three chief Ulema are the Grand Mufti, the head of the Al-Azhar University and the Grand Kazi.

The Mufti is the principal law-doctor, he is authorised to issue fatawas, and like the Ottoman Mufti he wields great powers. It is related that Abbas I requested the Grand Mufti Sheikh Abbasi to issue a fatwa declaring that the power of ratifying a sentence of death lay not as was the customary practice with the Ottoman Sultan, but with the Khedive. The Grand Mufti refused to comply with the request. Thereupon Abbas I exiled him to Sudan but in the face of strong outburst of public protest the Mufti was recalled[1]. The grand Kazi was appointed till 1907 by the Ottoman Sultan direct from Constantinople.[2] He pronounced final judgments on all subjects affecting the personal status of the Muslims.

---

1. Earl Cromer, Modern Egypt, Vol. II, p. 174.

2. Ibid, p. 176.

In 1884 to the Earl of Northbrook, G.C.S.I., M. Samee Ullah, Khan Bahadur, C.M.G. submitted a report on the admininistration of Justice in Egypt. I quote below from Leaves from the Diary to an attache to the Earl of Northbrook (Nawab Sarbuland Jung Bahadur.) "There were four other judges besides Mr. Sheldon-Amos on the bench the chief being Ismail Yousuf Pacha........
The proceedings were rather tedious. Father (M. Samee Ullah Khan) sat with the judges. Several criminal cases were heard....Men were brought before the court and after some preliminary questions.... The witnesses were brought before the court and put in the witness-box and all together and the usual questions asked....The advocates pleaded. Case over Judgment to be delivered after all the cases had been heard, p. 13. Here is a detail account on p. 24.—From a crimin-

Egypt has now a new constitution, a legislative assembly with the Khedive as the King of Egypt. The government is too much absorbed in internal affairs and politics to devote itself to judicial reforms.

---

al case shown by Chefik Bey, the Procureur-General. "On February 20th a fellow was arrested by a police constable who took him to the Inspector who took down a brief account..This would be called the accusation. Then the Mudir writes a note on the report of the police and sends it to the Procureur who..sents it on..to the Judge d'Instruction. There the accused and witnesses are summoned and examined. Medical opinion duly taken....The Judge d'Instruction sends the case back to the Procureur....The Procureur informs the prisoner that he will be tried on such and such a date (17th March). The Procureur endorses his opinion and demands the verdict of the court of First Instance, a tribunal composed of three Judges. The case is brought before the court (2nd examination of witnesses). Then comes the sentence of 3 years imprisonment (2nd April)....The case goes to the Appellate Court....One Judge out of 5 is allowed, about three days or so, to get up the case and to give an idea of it to his colleagues at the sitting. Judgment. The case thus lasted from February 20th to 22nd July."

VIII
THE ADMINISTRATION OF JUSTICE OF THE MUSLIM LAW IN PERSIA

Political history.

The Muslim connection with the great Kingdom of Persia began in 628 A. D. when the Prophet of Islam sent a letter to the Great King Khusru son of Hormuzd.[1] But it was in 633 A. D. during the Khilafat of Abu Bakr that the famous Muslim General Khalid started the campaign against Persia. However he was soon called upon to meet the Byzantine army and this incident saved Persia. It was during the reigns of Umar and Usman that the Empire of Khusru's was annexed and Ibn-A-amir, the Governor of Basra extended Muslim dominion to Kabul, Sistan and Kerman provinces. The Persians willingly received Islam and in turn asserted their intellectual superiority over the Arabs.[2] For long Persia was governed as a province by the Umayyad Khalifas till the Abbaside threw over the Umayyad Dynasty.

---

1. The text of the letter was as follows.

"In the name of Allah the Merciful and Compassionate. From Muhammad, the apostle of God to Khusru King of Iran, with greetings to the faithful who believe in God and His Apostle. I speak forth and witness that there is no God but God, He is alone and without associate and Muhammad is His servant and Apostle, and I send you the message of God as I am His messenger for the people. The object of my mission is to remind those whose Hearts are sincere and for the unbelievers to believe. If you accept Islam you will be happy and if you reject it you will be a sinner."

بسم الله الرحمن الرحيم

من محمد رسول الله الى
كسرى عظيم فارس سلام على من
اتبع الهدى و امن بالله و رسوله
و اشهد ان لا اله الا الله وحده
لا شريک له و ان محمداً عبده و
رسوله و ادعوک بدعاء الله فاني
رسول الله الى الناس كافة لانذر
من كان حيا و يحق القول على
الكافرين فاسلم تسلم فان ابيت
فان اثم المجوس عليک۔

2. E. G. Browne. A Literary History of Persia, Book III, Vol. I. p. 251.

The Abbaside had owed their success to the armies raised in Khorassan but as the result of weakness in the Abbaside Khalifa's new independent dynasties grew up in Persia.[1] However in 1258 A. D. the great conqueror Hulaku Khan sacked Baghdad for a week[2] executed the Khalif Mustasim Billah and thus became the undisputed ruler of Persia and established the Mongol dynasty.[3]

The national History of Persia commences from the establishment of the Safavi dynasty by Ismail in A. D. 1499, and finally Shah Abbas the Great formed in Persia a stable Government. In A. D. 1722 the Safavi dynasty was destroyed by Mahmud Ghilzais of Kandhar. In A. D. 1736 the great Asiatic Conqueror Nadir Shah was crowned King of Iran. The recent Kajar dynasty was founded by Muhammad Khan in A. D. 1796. Ahmad Shah the last King of the Kajar dynasty who had ascended the throne of Persia on July 28th, 1914 was deposed by the Persian Mejliss on 31st October, 1925, in the name of national welfare.[4] Later on the Constituent Assembly elected Riza Khan Pehlevi as the new Shah of Persia.[5]

Administration of justice

The introduction of Islam in Persia did not materially change the constitution of the Government and the administration of Justice. When the democratic principles of Islam were within its ownfold replaced by absolute monarchy, it is the least to say that it had not exercised much influence in far distant lands.

---

1. The Tahiri dynasty, the Saffar dynasty, the Samanid dynasty, the Buwayhid dynasty, and the Ghazna dynasty.

2. It is alleged that one million inhabitants were massacred.

3. The reigns of Ghazan Khan and Tamerlane are noteworthy.

4. The Pioneer, November 4th, 1925.

5. The Pioneer, December 14th, 1925.

Riza Khan comes from Mauzendran and traces his descent from the ancient Sassanian Kings. Another report says that he was a mere peasant boy.

The King of Persia combines in himself the threefold judicial, legislative and executive functions. Malcolm observes, "The Monarch of Persia has been pronounced one of the most absolute in the world; and it has been shown that there is reason to believe his condition has been the same from the most early ages........It is a maxim in that nation, that the King can do what he chooses, and that he is completely exempt from responsibility. He can appoint and dismiss ministers, judges, and officers of all ranks. He can also seize the property, or take away the life of any of his subjects......The ecclesiastical class, which includes the priests who officiate in the offices of religion, and those who expound the law as laid down in the Koran and the books of traditions, are deemed by the defenceless part of the population, as the principal shield between them and the absolute authority of the monarch."[1] Hence the law of Persia like that of all Muslim countries is directly based upon the Koran and the Hadises, and in fact the priests in the capacity of administrators of the Sacred law were in some degree natural protectors of the people. According to the strict theory of Islam, there should be no other courts of justice except the courts of Kazis which is sanctioned by the law, but in Persia as likewise in India and other countries it was not possible to reject the customary law which was not inconsistent with the Sacred Muslim law. The Persians did not sacrifice their own traditional laws and usages, and while they submitted to indispensable Islamic ordinances they preserved their own system of government and laws. Consequently there were two distinct judicial courts working side by side in Persia. The division was natural the Kazi courts were called upon to take cognizance of disputes about mariage dower, divorce, sale and almost all civil cases, while the customary courts preserved jurisdiction in respect of murder, theft, fraud and other crimes.

1. Sir John Malcolm. The History of Persia, Vol. II, p. 431.

The head Persian priest or judge was known as the "Sudder-ul-Sudder." He was appointed by the Sovereign and he nominated with the approbation of the Sovereign all chief Judges of the kingdom. The Sudder-ul-Sudder exercised great power and Shah Abbas the great on the death of the last chief Sudder intentionally refrained from nominating his successor. Shah Suffee appointed two different persons (Sudder-ul-Suddur-i-khas and Sudder-ul-Suddur i-am) to carry out the same work.. However Nadir Shah abolished the post altogether.[1] The mujtahids[2] have always existed in Persia and after the abolition of the post of the Priest they came into more prominence. The ecclesiastical order owes its reputation to the fact that it elects not to connect themselves with the Government or the people. The mujtahids were frequently consulted by the civil Judges, who were bound to respect their interpretation of the Shera. The King appoints a Sheikh-ul-Islam in every principal city, and he receives a liberal salary. In large cities there is a Kazi who is immediately subordinate to the Sheikh-ul-Islam. In small town there was a "moolah" only who could refer difficult points to the Kazi and thereby to the Sheikh-ul-Islam for decision. There is also a post of Mufti in Persia whose duty is to aid and advise the courts, and his opinion often influences their decisions.

Customary Court.

The King, his lieutenants, governors, and lay magistrates administered the customary law. They were prompt and arbitrary in their decisions.[3] The injured party was allowed to appeal to the superior officer. The power to inflict the punishment of death is not delegated by the King except to the Governors

1. Sir John Malcolm. The History of Persia, Vol. II, p. 440.

2. There are mujtahids in India also.

3. "The administration of the customary law or urf is more summary than that of Sherrah, because it is more arbitrary." Malcolm J. History of Persia, p. 450.

of the blood royal. There is a distinction between the modern and the ancient theory of punishment. Now it is the right of the state to punish, then it was the privilege of the Kins of the murdered person either to inflict the punishment of death or compound it. Thus theft may be forgiven and murder compounded. Malcolm says, "The barbarous usage of committing the execution of the law into the hands of the injured individual is still practised in Persia. It is only a few years ago that the English resident at Abusheher saw three persons delivered into the hands of the relations of those whom they had murdered."[1] The common mode of inflicting the punishment of death in Persia was by strangling by decapitation or by stabbing, and in some case, to gratify revenge excessive cruelty is applied. Women are seldom publicly executed and that may be because of their status in society.

During the reign of the Safavi dynasty the Court of Supreme criminal Judge was known as "Dewan Beggee". This Court administered Justice not only in the metropolis, but his jurisdiction extended all over the Kingdom, and it took cognizance in particular of four crimes, murder, rape, knocking of a trooth or an eye, other crimes were judged by the "Haukim or Chief Magistrate[2] of the place where they were committed. However it was the privilege of the nobles and ambassadors to have every suit they instituted or that was filed against them, tried in the court of "Dewan Beggee". This court no longer exists, its powers are now vested in the King and are exercisable by one of the royal heirs acting as governor in a province.

---

1. The Hrstory of Persia, p. 451 and on p. 462. "It is very usual for the heir of a person who has been murdered to demand not only goods and horses, but one or more of the nearest female relations of the murderer in marriage and this is deemed the best of all modes of ending the feud........... "

2. He also refers all Civil suits for trial and decisions to the Courts of Shera.

The Islamic law has prescribed definite punishment for each crime, but the customary courts do not administer shera, and thus the sentences pronounced by the persons in power varies according to their will and gravity of the offence. Fines, flogging and bastinado are usual punishments. Torture is sometimes applied, the taking out of the eye was a special kind of punishment, "the object of this barbarity are usually persons who have aspired to, or are supposed likely to aspire to the throne," and sometimes it is inflicted upon chief of tribes and to rebels.[1]

The King nominates all the officers "Beglerbegs" or provincial Governors; Haukims or Governors of cities, Darogah or Lieutenant of Police, but though the Kalanter Chief Magistrate of the city and the Kutkhodahs, Magistrates of different wards are nominated by the King, they are usually the most respectable citizens of the place where they are appointed. It was the general practice to pay the officers by assignments on the public revenue of different provinces. The whole administration of justice especially of the district near the capital is centralised in the person of the King, and Malcolm observes, "the King of Persia always exercises his power as the chief Magistrate of the Urf, or customary law, in his own capital, and the districts surrounding it, and all Civil and Criminal Cases, after being examined by subordinate officers of justice, are submitted to him for decisions........the inhabitants of the capital, who are under the immediate jurisdiction of the monarch, are the happiest and the best governed."[2]

---

1. Malcolm J., the History of Persia, p. 453.
2. Ibid, p. 484.

THE ADMINISTRATION OF JUSTICE OF MUSLIM LAW IN INDIA

Sindh under the Arabs.

In A. D. 712, the famous Muslim General Muhammad Qasim defeated Rai Dahir and annexed Sindh and Multan.[1] At this time the Arabs very wisely left the internal administration of the country in the hands of the Indians. The same Brahmans who occupied important administrative positions in the time of Rai Dahir were called upon to hold the great offices and discharge, their duties. Mohammad Qasim had absolute confidence in their integrity and honesty. Wida, son of Hamidun[2] Najdi was the first Muslim Governor of Brahmanabad. Of this period, we can say that the Muslim Law was not the national Law of the land. However the Muslim soldiers were bound by the Shera of Islam and had their own Civil Judges, Kazis and Muftis.

Subuktigin and Mahmud.

Subuktigin was the first Muslim to invade India from the North-west. His two invasions were like passing storms. He died in A. D. 999. His son Mahmud of Ghazni from A. D. 999—1030 had overrun from the Indus to the Ganges, but Mahmud's invasions were a failure. He did not establish a stable Government. Of this period we have no record of the Muslim administration of Justice in India.

Muhammad Ghori and the slave King 1173—1290.

The permanent conquest of India dates from the victories of Muhammad Ghori. In 1192 Muhammad defeated the Rajputs under Prithvi Raj and captured Delhi. His chief Viceroy in India began the famous Slave dynasty which lasted from A. D. 1206-1290. Aybak was the first slave King. His successor Altamish

1. The Province of Sindh and Multan yielded about 11,500,000 dirhams annually.

2. H. M. Elliot History of India, Vol. I, p. 183.

was styled Aid of the commander of the Faithful *Nasir-Amir-ul-Muminin.* The greatest of the slave Kings was Balban.[1]

The administration of Justice was carried out by the Kazis with the help of the Muftis as was common in other Muslim Countries. The Chief Judge at the time of Aybek was Sharful-Mulk.[2] Hasan Nizami says of Kutub-uddin Aybek " He extinguished the flame of discord by the splendour of the light of Justice."

Sultan Balban established a very strong Government. He was himself interested in the administration of Justice. He never showed any partiality towards any of his subjects even if they were his kin and relations. Balban also established a system of espionage with a view to make the administration of justice efficient; the spies were called upon .to report every act of misconduct and every instance of miscarriage ot Justice to the Monarch directly. It is related that when Malik Barbak one of his chief courtiers caused a servant to be scourged to death, and the deceased's widow complained to Balban, the Sultan ordered Malik Barbak to be flogged similarly in the presence of the widow. The spies for failure of reporting the case to the Sultan were instantly executed.[3]

The old system of the Muslim Law that to escape the penalty of debt the accused may compound with the relations of the deceased was in practice at that time. There is an instance where a nobleman was allowed to compound on the payment of 20,000 tankas.[4]

---

1. "Balban, the slave, water carrier, huntsman, general, statesman and Sultan is one of the most striking figures among many notable men in the long line of the Kings of Delhi." S. Lane Pooie, Mediæval India, p. 88.

2. Taj-ul-Maasir by Hasan Nizami. H. M. Elliot, History of India, Vol. I, p. 208.

3. Ishwari Prashad. History of Medieval India, p. 160.

4. Ibid, p. 161

The throne of Delhi was now held by the Khalji Turks.

The Khalji dynasty 1290-1321.

Sultan Alauddin was the greatest King, of that dynasty. The Sultan was opposed to ecclesiastical interference in matters of law and religion.[1] On several occasions as regards the application of the sacred law there was a conflict of opinion between the Sultan and Kazi Mughis-uddin. Once the Sultan questioned the Kazi thus "The wealth acquired at Deogir belongs to me or to the Treasury, Bait-ul-mal." Mughis-uddin replied "Your Majesty, according to the Law, as the treasure was acquired by the Muslim army it belongs to the public Treasury." Alauddin was annoyed and put the next question "what rights have I and my heirs upon the public Treasury." The Kazi answered "if your Majesty wants to follow the example set by the great Khalifas then your Majesty may rightfully take a sum which you have alloted to each fighting-man, or to each chief officer or your Majesty may draw any sum suitable for maintaining legitimate expenditure, but for any additional useless expenses your Majesty will be answerable to God." Kazi Ala-ul-Mulk was another great personality. He was consulted by the Sultan when he intended to set out for a world conquest, and to establish a new religion. The Kazi advised the Sultan to confine his military ambitions to India only. "Religion and law" said the Kazi, "spring from heavenly revelations. They cannot be established by the plans and designs of monarchs." The administration of Justice during the reign of Alauddin was satisfactory, but it rapidly declined under his weak and unfit successors, Mubarak Shah and Khusru Khan.

The Tughlaq dynasty 1321-1413.

Ghazi Malik "the trusty warden of the marches" ascended the throne of Delhi in 1320 A. D. He was a vigorous King. His son and successor Muhammad Tughlaq is styled "the man of

1. "The Law was to depend upon the will of the monarch and had nothing to do with the law of the Prophet." Ishwari Prashad. History of Medieval India, p 207.

ideas." He is the most striking figure in the history of India. Muhammad Tughlaq was a just monarch. He made himself the Supreme Court of Appeal.[1] And whenever the ends of justice demanded he overruled the Kazis and Muftis [2] of the court. He also appointed distinguished officers of the state as Judges irrespective of the fact whether they were professed Ulema or not. Ibn Batuta speaks very highly of the Sultan, in his opinion "of all men this King is the most humble ; and of all men h· most loves justice[3]. In A. D. 1333 Ibn Batuta was also appointed Kazi of Delhi by Muhammad Tughlaq. Ibn Batuta lived in India for about eight years. He left India in A. D. 1342. The eight cases of murde· of theologians. Sheikhs and Maulvis mentioned by Ibn Batuta are of those who had misappropriated public funds or participated in seditious movements. The Sultan submitted to the decrees of the court passed against himself.[4] The notable Kazi of this period was Kazi Kamal-uddin Sadr-i-Jahan.

The successor of Muhammad Tughlaq Firoz was a pious and merciful King he abolished the torture which

---

1. Al-Badaoni says (Muntakhabu-t-Tawarikh translated by G. S. Ranking, p. 317) "that he (Sultan) used to keep four Muftis to whom he alloted quarters in the precincts of his own place,....so that when anyone who was arrested upon any charge, he might in the first place argue with the Muftis about his due punishment....and he said, 'Be very careful that you do not fail in the slightest degree by defect in speakir·· that which you consider right, because if anyone should be pu death wrongfully the blood of that man will be upon your head. Then if after long discussion they convicted (the prisoner) even though it were midnight he would pass orders for his execution."

2. Ibid, p. 311.

3. Ibn Batuta Parised III, p. 285-86.

4. Al-Badaoni, p. 318, mentions, that once Sultan Muhammad Tughlaq went on foot and filed a case against Sheikhzada-i-Jami for accusing him as a Tyrant. The Sheikhzada was bold enough to confess the statement and told the Sultan that he was wrong in handing over wife and children of the man sentenced to death to the executioners, as he was accustomed to do.

was the common form of punishment.[1] Firoz died in A. D. 1388. During the reigns of the rest of the monarchs of this dynasty the administration of Justice was not so perfect. The invasion of Timur occurred during the reign of Mahmud Shah and his rival Nasrat Shah.

Timur's invasion, A. D. 1398.

Timur is the greatest of the world conquerors. He was born in A. D. 1336 at Kelh in Transoxiana. The history of the military adventures of this great Muslim conqueror is interwoven with the entire history of Islam. He shattered all the Muslim Asiatic monarchies into pieces. The fate of the Delhi Empire was similar to the fate of the Turkish Empire of the great Bajazet. Timur crossed the Indus on September 24, A. D. 1398, sacked Delhi where he remained for a fortnight, and after a brilliant series of victories he eventually left for Samarcund. The Government of Delhi was paralysed, the process of disintegration had set in and small states came into existence all over India.[2]

The Saiyyids (1414-1415) and the Lodis (1451-1526.)

The reigns of the Saiyyids and the Lodis are not of much importance; Sultan Sikandar Lodi was a notable exception. He restored the machinery of civil administration to some extent. The Chief Judge, during his reign was known as Mir-i-adal and this office was held by the jurist Mian Bhua.[3]

A distinguished jurist of this period was, Sheikhul. Hadayah of Jaunpore. He wrote commenteries on the Hedayah i-Fiqh; which is a celebrated book of Muslim Jurisprudence.[4] The other great jurists were, Sheikh Adbd-ullah Tulumbi and Sheikh Aziz-ullah Tulumbi who introduced a systematic study of Logic and jurisprudence. The Judicial and administrative reforms initiated by Sultan

1. Ishwari Prasad History, Medieval India, p. 287.

2. Jaunpore (1394) Gujarat (1397) and Malwa (1401) became independent Kingdoms.

3. Tabakat-i-Akbari Persian text, p.173.

4. Al-Badaoni, p. 428.

Sikandar Lodi were the basis of the administrative machinery set up so effectually by Sher Shah.

Sher Shah Sur dynasty 1539—1555.

After the defeat of the Emperor Humayun Sher Shah ascended the throne of Delhi. He was one of the greatest figures of medieval India. He was a great Administrator. During the short period of his reign which lasted for about five years and six months he considerably improved the administration of the country.

Sher Shah's predecessors had copied the Abbasides Khalifas in establishing state departments. The following were the chief departments.

(1) Diwan-i-Wizarat.

(2) Diwan-i-ariz the Army department.

(3) The Intelligence department created by Sultan Balban.

(4) The Judiciary under the Chief Kazi also known as Dad-bak,[1] Chief administratior of Justice. Firoz Tughluq had also placed State industries, public works and royal mint under a diwan wazir.

Sher Shah considerably improved the working of all departments. His ministers were mere Secretaries called arkan-i-adaulat. He made the pargana as the administrative unit without destroying the autonomous village communities. He appointed a Shiqdar, a amin, and one fotahdar the treasure and two Karkuns-writers. The Shiqdar was a entrusted with police duties. The amin was responsible for civil work, for the assessment and collection of revenue. The treasurer and karkuns were subordinate to the amin. The next unit planed by Sher Shah was the Sarkar.[2] The officers responsible for the administration of the Sarkar

1. H. M Elliot, History of India, Vol. III, p. 126 Malik Nizamuddin was Dad-bak and Naib-i-mulk, deputy ruler of the state during the reign of Kai-Kubad.

2. During The reign of Akbar "the Empire was divided into 105 Sarkars." A Beveridge Emperor Akbar, Vol. I, p. 265.

were the Chief Shiqdar, Shiqdar-i-Shiqdaran[1], and the Chief Munsif, Munsif-Munsifan. The Chief Munsif was responsible for the civil administration, and he acted as a circuit Judge for trying civil cases. The Shiqdar administered Criminal justice according to the Shera of Islam. The muquddams of the village were responsible to produce the offenders and it is related that if the muquddams, where a murder had taken place, failed to produce the offender they were themselves put to death.[2] So stern was Justice that it became proverbial that Sher Shah turned robbers and thieves into guardians of peace. The civil Judges were not necessarily canon-lawyers. According to al-Badaoni comprehensive instructions on all important points of religion and civil administration were issued to all the Sarkars. " All these points were written in these documents whether agreeable to the religious Law or not ; so that there was no necessity to refer any such matters to the Qazi or Mufti, nor was it proper to do so."[3] Thus we see that the administration of Muslim law was being modified to suit the requirements of that age. Sher Shah was called the Sultan-ul-Adal, the Just monarch. He named his eldest son Adil Khan the Just Lord, and there is a well known story about Adil Khan related in the khulasa-at-Tawarikh The Prince threw a *bira* of pan on a citizen's wife while she was bathing in the river, the woman resented this conduct of the prince, and her husband complained of it to the Sultan. The monarch declared that the Law of retaliation was to be enforced, that is, the citizen shall throw a *bira* on to the prince's wife in the same manner.[4] Kazi Fazilat was judge in the army of Sher Shah.

---

1. The chief Shiqdar had about 2,000 to 5,000 troopers. He resembled the faujdar appointed by the Mughals. The Subahs, and Subahaders were the creation of Akbar. 2. K. Qanungo Sher Shah, p. 396.

3. Al-Badaoni, p. 496. This was the state of affairs during the reign of Islam Shah. 4. W. Erskine, History of India. p. 443.

XI
THE ADMINISTRATION OF JUSTICE BY THE MUGHAL EMPERORS

It was in A. D. 1526 that Shah Babar invaded India and established a famous dynasty which represents the Golden Age of the Muslim rule in Hindustan. His reign was brief.[1] His son the Emperor Humayun was unfortunate in being defeated by the great Afghan ruler, Sher Shah at the battle of Chaunsa and at the battle of Ganges in May 1540. However in A. D. 1555, Humayun defeated Sikandar at Sirhind, and once more found himself in possession of the throne of Delhi. Al-Badaoni speaks highly of this monarch, and as the most orthodox of the Muslim Kings.[2] During his reign the influence of the Ulemas revived. The judicial reforms made by Sher Shah had survived and remained intact.

Akbar.

A drastic change occurred during the reign of the Emperor Akbar. It was apparently a reversal of the policy of Islam,[3] and this era marks the downfall of the Ulemas. The institution of the religion "Din-i-Ilahi" and the conferences held in the Ibadat Khan completely shattered the orthodox Sunni school. Akbar believed himself to be a divine head and King[4]. According to the Muslim view the

---

1. Khwjah A. Marwarid was sometime the Sadar and the jurist Ekhtiar was the Kazi, Memoirs of Baber, p. 189. (tr. by T. Leyden and W. Erskine.)

2. Al-Badaoni (Ranking) Vol. I, p. 602. "He never remained for an instant without the *Muza* nor did he ever take the name of God nor of the Prophet may the peace and blessing of God be upon him with out Tiharat."

3. Al-Badaoni says (Ranking) Vol. II, p. 324. "During those days the public prayers and *Azan*....was abolished."

4. Abul Fazal says in the Ain (Blochmann I, c. p. 111) "Royalty is a light emanating from God, and a ray from the sun, the illuminator of the universe, the argument of the book of perfection, the respectable of all virtues......In his wisdom, the King well understand the spirit of the age......when he performs an action, he considers God as the real doer of it."

Ulemas and the Mujtahids are the custodians of the Shera of Islam. Akbar tried to usurp the highest power to mould the law also. An Imperial decree was published in A. D. 1579 which was signed by Sheikh Abdunabi the Chief Justice, by the Sadr-i-Jahan, Kazi Jalaluddin, Makhdum-ul-Mulk Ghazi Khan and by other Ulemas, as well as by Sheikh Mubarak who was the instigator of this idea to Akbar. The decree conferred on the Emperor the Spiritual headship of the Empire.[1] The Emperor became the sole Judge of final appeal. The Ulemas put up a fight but all in vain. Makhdum-ul-Mulk and Shaikh Abdunabi were banished, sent to Mecca, and Sultan Khwajah who joined the Din-i-Ilahi was made Sadr-i-Jahan, (1578-1585).

---

1. The decree runs as follows. Blochmann I, c. p. 186-7, Beveridge, Emperor Akbar p. 318-19. Al-Badaoni, Vol. II, p, 279, "where Hindustan has now become the centre of security and peace, and the law of justice and beneficience......now we, the principal, Ulema who are not only well versed in the several departments of the law and in the principles of jurisprudence......have duly considered the deep meaning of the verse of the Qoran (Sur IV, 62) 'obey God and obey the prophet, and those who have authority among you"........we have agreed that rank of a Sultan-i-Adil (a just ruler) is higher in the eye of God than the rank of a Mujtahid. Further we declare that the King of the Islam........Jalaluddin Muhammad Akbar, is a most just, a most wise and a most God fearing King. Should therefore, in future a religious question come up regarding which the opinions of the Mujtahids are at variance and his Majesty, in his penetrating understanding and clear wisdom, be inclined to adopt for the benefit of the nation, and as a political expedient any of the conflicting opinions which exist on that point, and issue a decree to that effect, we do hereby agree that such a decree shall be binding on us and on the whole nation. Further we declare that, should His Majesty think fit to issue a new order, we and the nation shall likewise be bound by it, provided always that such an order be not only in accordance with some verse of the Qoran, but also of real benefit for the nation ; and further that any opposition on the part the subjects to such an order as passed by His Majesty, shall involve damnation in world to come and loss of religion and property in this life."

The following were the famous judges during the reign of Akbar.[1]

Maulana Abdullah of Sultanpur known as Makhdum-ul-Mulk and Sheikh-ul-Islam.

Kazi Yaqub of Manikpur.

Kazi Jalaluddin of Multan.

Kazi Tawa'isi.

Kazi Sadruddin sometime of Jalandhar and Lahore.

Kazi Mubarak of Gopamau.

Kazi Nurullah of Shustar.

Kazi Abul'l Ma'Ali.

Kazi Nizam of Badakshan

Sheikh Abunabi Sadr-i-Jahan.

Sheikh Mubarak Sadr-i-Jahan.

Mir Sayyid Muhammad Mir-i-adl.

Maulana Muhammad Mufti.

In A. D. 1605 the Emperor Jahangir ascended the throne of Delhi. Jahangir revised the policy of Akbar. Inspite of his vices he professed himself a Muslim, he restored the Muhammadan formulas of faith and even revived the Hijra chronology. He took keen interest in the administration of Justice. It is said that with a view to redress the grievances of the people, he had a chain and bell attached to his royal apartment, and one end of the chain was fastened to a tower at the bank of the Jumna.[2] The Emperor frequently sat in the royal court to hear petitions.[3] Jahangir interdicted the cutting of noses and ears,[4] and the death penalty could not be inflicted without the permission and confirmation of the Emperor.

---

1. Al-Badaoni (Ranking) Vol. III, Chapter II, 109.

2. Rogers and Beveridge, 17.

"I ordered them to make a chain of gold thirty gaz in length and containing sixty bells. Its weight was six Indian maunds........one end of it they made fast to the battlements of the Shah Burj of the fort at Agra and the other to a stone post fixed on the bank of the river."

3. Beni Prasad, History of Jahangir, p. 110.

4. Institutes of Jahangir, Art. 5, H. M. Elliot, History of India, Vol. VI, p. 503.

This view is supported by Monsieur Thevenot.[1] "From Terry and Roe however it is clear that the provincial Viceroys passed and executed sentences of death".[2]

The reign of Shah Jahan is notable for peace and prosperity. The French traveller Tavernier speaks of the reign of Shah Jahan as like that of a father over his family[3], and bears witness to the just administration of Justice. Shah Jahan being a pious Muslim abolished the ceremony of prostration which was directly against Islamic injunctions. Shah Jahan himself heard petitions, and fixed Wednesday as the day for the administration of Justice.[4] The Emperor established a regular system of appeals. From the court of first instance an appeal could be filed in the court of the Governor or in the court of Kazi of Subha. "If parties were not satisfied even with these decisions they appealed to the Chief Diwan or to the Chief Kazi on matters of law."[5]

Aurangzib.

In A. D. 1659 Aurangzib ascended the throne of Delhi; he is well-known as Alamgir, the "World-compeller". He was a stern puritan monarch. Aurangzib's ideal of enlightened kingship can be gathered from his own sayings. He wrote to Shah Jahan thus, "Soveregnity is the guardianship of the people not self-indulgence and profligacy." He was fond of reciting the following couplets of Sadi, "Cease to be Kings! Oh, Cease to be Kings! or determine that your dominions shall

---

1. The Travels of Monsieur de Thevenot III. ch. X, p. 19. "All sentences of death passed whether by civil or criminal judges had to wait for execution until the Emperor's confirmation was obtained."

2. Beni Prasad, History of Jahangir, p. 113. A Monserrate says (Tr. Hosten J., Asiatic Society of Bengal, VIII, 1912, p. 194) that "whenever the Emperor was present the death penalty could not be inflicted without his sanction."

3. H. M. Elliot, History of India, Vol. VII, p. 170.

4. Ibid, p. 172.

5. Ibid, p. 173.

be governed only by yourselves." "Ovington speaks of the Emperor as "the ocean of justice."[1]

The author of Muntakhab-ul-lubhab pays a tribute to Aurangzib, "of all the sovereigns of the house of Timur, nay of all the Sovereigns of Delhi no one since Sikander Lodi, has ever been apparently so distinguished for devotion, austerity and justice."[2]

Aurangzib was well acquainted with the Hadis and other standard books on fiqha. He was a great jurist. He had committed the Koran to memory[3]. In A. D. 1565 the Emperor ordered for the compilation of the celebrated code the Fatawa-i-Alamgiri. The Chief compiler of the Alamgiri was Sheikh Nizam[4] and Chulpi 'Abdullah, son of Maulana 'Abdul Hakim of Sialkot was ordered to translate the work into Persian. This book contains all the essential principles of the Hanafi system of jurisprudence.

The following were the Chief State departments.

1. "The Exchequer and Revenue (under the High *Diwan*).

2. The Imperial Household (under the *Khan-i-saman* or High Steward).

3. The Military pay and accounts office (under the Imperial *Bakshi*).

4. Canon law, both civil and criminal (under the Chief *Kazi*).

1. Voyage to Surat in the year 1689, p. 198.

S. Lane Poole, Medieval India, p. 365.

"No act of injustice according to the law of Islam, at least after his accession has been proved against him."

2. H. M. Elliot, History of India, Vol. VII, p. 386.

3. Masir-i-Alamgiri. 531-532 (J. N. Sarkar, History of Aurangzib, Vol. I, p. 7) "His favourite study was theological works—Commenatries on the Quran, the Traditions of Muhammad Canon law, the works of Imam Muhammed Ghazzali, selections from the letters of Shaikh sharf Yahia of Munir and Shaikh Zainuddin Outb Muhi Shirazi and other works of that class."

4. H. M. Elliot, History of India, Vol. VII, p. 160.

5. Religious endowments and charity (under the Chief *Sadr*).

6. Censorship of public morals (under the *Muthasib*)."[1]

We are mainly concerned with the last three departments which were responsible for the administration of Justice.

King's Court.

The Mughal Emperor like his contemporary monarchs of Turkey and Persia posed as the fountain of Justice and followed the immemorial tradition that the King in person should try cases in open Court. The Emperor sat in the *Diwan-i-khas* trying cases. The Court of the Emperor was the highest Court of Appeal, the Supreme tribunal of the land. The Imperial Court consisted of the Emperor himself, the Kazis[2] Muftis[3] and Adils[4]. The Darogha-i-adalat[5] and the Kotwal[6] were required to be present.

Several early European travellers have left a picturesque account of the trials held by the Mughal Emperors.

In A. D. 1511 William Finch writes.

"The Castle of Agra has four gates........one to the west...... is called the kachari gate, within which, over against the great gate is the Kazis seat of Chief justice. Over against this seat is the Kachari or Courts of Rolls where the King's Wazir sits every morning ......Tuesday is day of blood, both of fighting beasts and justiced men, the King judging and seeing execution." (Purchas IV, 72, 73).

Bernier, an eye-witness describes how the Emperor Aurangzib administered Justice.

"All the petitions held up in the crowd assembled in the Hall of Public Audience are brought to the King and read in his hearing and the persons concerned being ordered to approach are examined by the monarch himself, who often redresses on the spot the wrongs of the aggrieved party". (Bernier, 263).

---

1. J. N. Sarkar, Mughal Administration, p. 22.

2. The Judges of sacred law Shera. 3. The jurists entitled to issue fatawas. 4. The Judges of common law. 5. The Superintendent of the Court. 6. The prefect of the police.

Manucci also gives an account of the Emperor administering Justice.

"The King holds public audience in the Amkhas, and there it is usual for aggrievd persons to appear and make complaint. Some men demand punishment for murderers, others complain of injustice and violence ....the King ordains....that the thieves be beheaded, that the governors and faujdars compensate the plundered travellers......In some cases he announces that there is no pardon for the transgressor, in others he orders the facts to be investigated and a report made to him." (Storia II, 462).

Kazi-ul-Kuzat.

The Supreme Kazi wes called the Kazi-ul-Kuzat, in every town he appointed a local Kazi.[1] The Kazis appointed in the Provinces were expected to work for five days in the week on Saturday, Sunday, Monday, Tuesday and thursday, while on Wednesday they were required to be present in the Subahdar's (Governor), Darbar. Friday was a holiday.[2]

The following is the list of the Chief Kazis during the reign of the Emperor Aurangzib.[3]

Abdul Wahhab Bohra	..	..	1659—1675
Sheikh-ul-Islam ..	..	..	1676—1683
Syed Abu Said ..	..	..	1683—1685
Khwaja Abdullah ..	..	..	1685—1698
Muhammad Akram .	..	..	1698—1706
Mullah Haidar ..	..	..June	1706—1707

During the reign of the Emperor Shah Jahan. Abdul Wahhab was the Kazi at Pattna. When the other Kazis had

---

1. A newly appointed judge was charged by the Kazi-ul-Kuzat as follows. "Be just, be honest be impartial. Hold trials in the presence of the parties and at the Court-house and the seat of Government muhakuma. "Do not accept presents......" "Write your decrees, sale-deeds, mortgage bonds and other legal documents very carefully, so that learned men may not pick holes in them and bring you to shame."

"Know proverty to be your glory". (J. N. Sarkar, Mughal Administration, p. 27.)

2. Mirat-i-Ahmadi, p. 291 the instructions issued by Aurangzib to the Governor of Gujrat.

3. J. N. Sarkar, History of Aurangzib, Vol. III, p. 81,

declined to declare Aurangzib's usurpation of the throne as valid, Abdul Wahhab asserted that as Shah Jahan was unfit to govern, the throne was virtually vacant and Aurangzib's accession was lawful. Thus Abdul Wahhab from the beginning became the Emperor's favourite. It is said that he was not a fit and proper person to hold this high post, he recklessly abused his influence to enrich himself.[1]

On the other hand Abdul Wahhab's scn Sheikh-ul-Islam is noted for his piety and integrity of character. " No such honest Kazi was ever again seen in India." This able Judge administered Justice to the entire satisfaction of the people. It is said he always tried his best to make the parties compound their dispute. Once the Emperor asked him whether he should set forth for the conquest of Golkonda and Bijapur. The learned Kazi did not hesitate in condemning the project as against the Koranic law for it was a war between two Muslim States."

Sadr.

The *Sadr* were the Civil Judge of the Empire. The Chief *Sadr* was called the *Sadr-us-Sadur* or the *Sadr-i-Jahan* and also *Sadr-i-kul.* His duty was to appoint in every province a local *Sadr.* The provincial *Sadrs* were instructed by the chief *Sadr* to maintain list of the recipients of rent-free lands and daily allowances. The Sadr was to see that these persons entitled to stipend carried out the Imperial orders. He also noted their deaths. Through the chief Sadr the Emperor distributed charity. It is stated that the chief Sadr spent one and a half laks of rupees annually during the month of Ramzan and likewise on other sacred festivals. During the reign of the Emperor the following were the Chief Sadrs.[2]

"Syed Hedayat-ullah Qadri	..	1658 Mar. 1660.
Shaikh Mirak of Herat ..	..	March, 1660—Nov, 1661.
Qalich Khan (Abidkh) ..	..	Nov. 1661—May 1667.

1. J. N. Sarkar, History of Aurangzib, Vol. III, p. 84.

2. Ibid, p. 81.

Razavi Khan ..	.. ..	May 1667—June, 1681.
Qalich Khan ..	.. ..	June 1681—Oct. 1682.
Sharif Khan ..	.. ..	Oct. 1681—Oct. 1682.
Fazil Khan II (Shaikh Makhdum)	..	Oct. 1682—Dec. 1688.
* ..	.. ..	1689—1698.
Qazi Abdullah............1698 (in addition to Chief Qazi-ship).		
Md. Amin Khan II (Chin Bahadur, Itimad-ud-Daula).		
..	.. ..	May 1698—1707."

The Sadr-us-Sadur was also responsible for the educational expenditure of the state. The teachers and maulavis were paid by the state. The students also received stipends on the recommendation of the teacher and the local provincial Sadr. Similarly the *Khankas*, theological institutions for education received subsidies from the state. All these expenses were met by the income of the Public Treasaury, Bait-ul-mal.

Censor.

The Muhtasib is the censor or inspector of the public morals. His duties were similar to the Muhtasib appointed by Umayyad or Abbaside Khalifas. He is responsible for public morals and to see that people did not indulge in sexual immorality or get intoxicated or gambled. He was also responsible for instructing the Muslims to perform the five daily prayers, and not to neglect the fast of Ramzan.

The following important instructions were given to a newly appointed censor in discharge of his quasi-judicial duties.[1]

"In the cities do not permit the sale of intoxicating drinks nor the residence of professional women as it is opposed to the sacred law."

"Give good counsel and warning to those who violate the Koranic precepts......"

"Fix the prices of good in the market and enforce the use of correct weights and measures."

"In the bazars and lanes if any one contrary to regulations and custom has srceneed off (abru) a part of the street, or closed the part or throwndirt and sweepings on the road......you should in such cases urge them to remove the violations of regulation."

---

*During this interval there is no record of the Sadrs in the Official History.

1. J. N. Sarkar, Mughal Administration, p. 30.

During the reign of Aurangzib the following held the office of censor[2]

Mullah Auz Wajih	.. ..	June, 1659 Oct. 1663.
Khwajah Qadir ..	.. ..	Oct. 1663 Oct. 1665.
Muhammad Zahid (son of Kazi Arslan)	..	Oct. 1665, 1668 or 1669.
Muhammad Husain Jaunpore	..	1668-March-1670.
Syed Amjad Khan	.. ..	Mar. 1670—1707.

Mullah Auz Wajih a native of Samarkand was the most noted Turani theologian in India. He came to India in A. D. 1640 and he was appointed Mufti by the Emperor Shah Jahan. In June 1659 the Emperor Aurangzib appointed him as the Chief Censor with the rank of a commander of one thousand horse. Some *Mansabdars* and Ahadis were placed under him to enforce his orders.

The power of the censor as the officer to enforce the Prophet's laws was supreme. In 1672 Muhammad Tahir Diwan of Hussan Ali Khan was beheaded at the intance of the censor for having cursed the first three Khalifas of Islam. In 1667 a Portuguese Friar who had accepted the Muslim faith reverted to his old faith again. In accordance with the Shera, on apostacy from Islam, he was put to death. The most notable trial of all was that of Sarmad, the eminent Sufi of Delhi[2]. His only fault was his nakedness which is against Islam. Aurangzib had warned him not to go about stark naked, but the great Sufi was obstinate.

He observed :

"He who invested thee with the King's crown.

Clad me all in the garb of distress.

He put dresses on all whom He saw sinful ;

On the sinless He conferred the robe of nakedness!"

Aurangzib's efforts were in vain, but the Puritan Emperor was not to be cowed. His respect for the personality of

1. J. N. Sarkar, History of Aurangzib, Vol. III, p. 81.

2. His grave is near Badshai Darwaza of the Juma Masjid, Delhi.

the great Sarmad could not persuade him to give up the Shera of Islam. He appointed a bench of Muslim theologians to sit in Judgment over Sarmad. Sarmad was condemned to death. The great Sufi as was fitting to his dignity only rejoiced, and said that his body had so long hindered the aspiration of his soul to present itself before God.[1]

The Kitab-Adab-ul-Kazi

The following is a summary from the Kitab Adab-ul-Kazi and Kitab-ul-Kuza, of the Fatawa-i-Alamgiri, the Durrul-Mukhtar and the Hedaya.

It is the duty of the Sultan to appoint a Kazi (who possesses the qualification of a witness), and the extent of his jurisdiction must be specified. The appointment may be subject to any lawful conditions. The Sultan may also appoint a Kazi-ul-Kuzat, the Chief Kazi. The Kazi-ul-Kuzat has the power to appoint and dismiss subordinate Kazis. According to Imam Abu Hanifa a Kazi ought not to be appointed for more than one year, and after a year had expired the Sultan ought to remove the Kazi, and ask him to devote himself to the study of law. He may be re-appointed again. The Kazi may receive a fixed salary from the Treasury, Bait-ul-Mal. The Kazi is to base his decisions on the Koran and the Hadis and then the Ijma of the Prophet's companions, and then on the Ijma of the Ulemas.

According to the Majmu-al-Nawazil the Kazi is not to try the case of a person to whom the Kazi bears enmity and ill-feeling. This was the opinion of Sheikh-ul-Islam Abul Hasan. In such a contingency the Kazi is to report to the Sultan to transfer the case to another Kazi. According to some jurists is such a case the Sultan may endorse his opinion on the decision of the Kazi. The Kazi is competent

1. It is wrong to attribute malicious motives to Aurangzib namely that he put Sarmad to death as the great Sufi was the favourite of Dara Shukoh.

to hear suits filed against the Sultan. Similarly the Sultan may himself file a case as plaintiff.[1]

According to the Hanafi Law a Kazi cannot pass an order in favour of his father, his mother, his child or his wife, but he can lawfully find against any of these relations,[2] because evidence against them is accepted on the ground that it is liable to no suspicion.[3]

For the administration of justice the Kazi is to sit in the central city mosque or in public Court, Dar-ul-Kuza, so that it may be convenient for the public to attend the Court. The Kazi when he enters the mosque should say his prayers first, and crave God's help in administering justice. The learned men of the city may sit near him. The Katib (writer) is to sit near the Kazi and the Kazi is to watch that the Katib records the evidence correctly. The superior officers on entering the Court may " wish salam " to the Kazi and the Kazi may reply in return, but he is not to take precedence in wishing, and similarly when a witness wishes "salâm to" the Kazi he is to reciprocate. The Kazi is to treat the parties (the plaintiff and defendant) on equal terms, they may be asked to sit in front of the Kazi. The Kazi's peons may be present at a distance in the Court. The Kazi is to take down the statement made by the plaintiff and then think over it, and should he be of opinion that the plaintiff's case is false, then he should call upon the plaintiff to support his case, but if the Kazi thinks in favour of the

---

1. The cases cited in support in the Fatawa-i-Alamgir are those of Umar in the court Zayd bin Sabit Ali in the court of Shurayh the Abbaside monarch Harun-ur-rashid in the court of Kazi Abu Yusuf.

2. Minhaj et-Talibin, p. 505 states the Shafi Law. A judgment delivered by a judge in his own favour, or in that of his slave, or of his partner in the same firm has no legal effect and similarly with a judgment in favour of his ancestors or descendants. In all these cases the judge......should refer the matter to the sovereign or to another judge."

3. C. Hamilton Hedaya (Grady), p. 344.

plaintiff he should ask the defendant to make his reply. After hearing the defendant the Kazi should ask his Katib to take down that on certain day, month and year the plaintiff, son of such a person filed a case against the defendant, son of such a person, and if necessary a short description of the plaintiff and of the defendant for identification purposes may be stated. If the defendant admits the claim, the Kazi should pass his judgment thereupon, but he denies then the evidence is to be tendered.

The plaintiff is called *Muddai* and the plaint is known as *dawa* "which is defined as a demand by a person of his right form another in the presence of a judge." The defendant is called *Muddai alaihi*. According to the Hedaya, "the *Moodaa* or plaintiff is a person who if he should voluntarily relinquish his claim cannot be compelled to prosecute it and the *Moodaa-alihee* or defendant, is a person who, if he should wish to avoid the litigation is compellable to sustain it."[1]

The *Muddai* can only be a person adult and possessed of understanding, hence a minor or a lunatic must file a claim through the intervention of a guardian, nor will a suit will be heard against such persons without such representation.

The following was the method adopted by the Kazis at the time of the Emperor Aurangzib, as reported in the Fatawa-i-Alamgiri.

The plaintiff presents himself in the Dar-ul-Kuza and goes to the Katib who writes out the plaint in the Court register, and enters the plaintiff's name his father's name and address, and also records the name of the Kazi in whose Court the plaint has been filed. The defendant's and his father's name and address is entered in the proper place leaving sufficient space to note down the defendant's reply.

1. C. Hamilton Hedaya (Grady), p. 399.

On the presentation of the case the Kazi goes through the record, the date of hearing is entered in the register, and the plaintiff or his Vakil presents the plaintiff's case, and the defendant is called upon to reply. If the defendant admits the claim, the case is decided accordingly, but if he denies it, then the plaintiff has two alternatives, he may put the defendant on oath[1] or produce evidence in support of his case. However if the plaintiff has his witnesses present in the Court, or is able to summon them, but still insists that the defendant should be put on oath, the better view is that Kazi is not to put the defendant on oath. The plaintiff cannot establish his case by taking an oath.[2]

The Kazi may either himself note down or ask the Katib to write name and address (and if necessary description of the witnesses) of the witnesses and take down a verbatim report of their depositions. It is better that the Kazi should himself take down the evidence, thereafter if the Kazi should be of opinion that the witnesses deposed correctly and in conformity with the plaint, then the Kazi is to ask the defendant as to what he has to say, and if the defendant requires time to support his case then it should be granted to him, otherwise the suit is to be decreed in favour of the plaintiff. The decision of the Kazi is to be noted down in the same register, or he may give a written order to the party who demands it. This is to prevent a fresh trial of the same

---

1. Minhaj et Talibin, p. 507. According to the Shafi-law, the judge before believing a witness evidence, unless he knows the person s character himself, should make a further enquiry through a *mozakki*.

2. C. Hamilton Hedaya, (Grady), p. 451.

"An oath cannot be exacted from the plaintiff because of the saying recorded in the traditions of the Prophet. 'Evidence is incumbent on the part of the appellant and an oath on that of the Respondent." Under the Shafii law the plaintiff may be put on oath Minhaj et Talibin, p. 508, ibid, p. 492. "An oath cannot be exacted from the defendant in claims respecting marriage divorce Aila bondage, Willa, punishment or Laan."

case on the same facts. A decree is defined as that which settles or terminates a dispute.

According to the Shafi-i-law judgment a may be passed *ex-parte* against the defendant[1]; and under the Hanafi Law, "the Kazi must not pass a decree against an absentee unless in the presence of his representative[2]."

According to the Fatawa-i-Alamgiri if the Kazi finds subsequently that the decree was in violation of the principles of Law, then he should review his previous judgment. However if he should find that there is merely a difference of opinion on the point which he has decided, then he ought not to interfere with his previous decision. The same view is found in the Shafi-i-law. "A judgment that subsequently appears to be at variance with a text of the Koran, with the Sonna, or with the general opinion of jurists, or with common sense should be quashed either by the judge who delivered it or by his colleague, substitutes or successors."[3]

The Muslim jurists differed on the point whether a Kazi may decide a case on his own personal knowledge. The accepted opinion is that if an incident took place in the Kazi's presence and he has ascertained it, and if the same matter is brought before him in the Court, then he may lawfully decide according to his personal knowledge.

When a decree has been passed by the Court, it can lawfully be executed. A judgment debtor can be compelled by imprisonment to comply with the provisions of the decree. In certain cases the defendant may set up a plea, in the nature of avoidance daf'â, for instance if a man claims a certain sum of money as a debt. The defendant may state that he owed the money, but he has paid it, or that the plaintiff has released him from the debt. The judge at the hearing of the case is also to see that the claim discloses a

---

1. Minhaj et Talibin, p. 507.
2. C. Hamilton Hedaya, (Grady), p. 342.
3. Minhaj et Talibin, p. 505.

good cause of action. In proper cases joinder of parties was possible Strictly speaking there is no law of limitation in the pure Muhammadan law, but periods of limitation for the hearing of suits may lawfully be laid down by the supreme ruler Khalifa or Sultan, as has been done in Turkey by the order of the Sultan. There is also a rule similar to *res judicata.* The same cause cannot be tried over again. A previous decree of the Kazi is conclusive and final. It can be tendered as evidence in the Court of law. The quasi-judicial duties of the Kazi are to superintend the jails, to supervise the trust, waqf properties, and to look after the interests of minors, lunatics and missing persons. The Kazi is to appoint an administrator to administer the estate of a deceased person, if the heirs are minors or are absent.

Arbitration.

The Muhammadan Law allows a case to be referred to an arbitrator for decision. The arbitrator must possess the essential qualities required for a Kazi [1]. However either party is allowed to retract before the award has been made by the arbitrator, but the moment it is given, it becomes binding upon them. If the parties refer the award to the Kazi, and if he were of the same opinion he might put the award into execution, as though it were the decree of the Court, but if the Kazi should be of the contrary opinion he might lawfully annul the award.

Similar to the decrees of a Kazi an award passed by the arbitrator in favour of his parent, wife and child is null and void. The parties who have acknowledged the arbitrator's award, are not allowed subsequently to retract from it. In certain cases no reference can be made to an arbitrator.[2]

---

1. C. Hamilton Hedaya, (Grady), p. 343.
" He must not be a slave, an infidel a slanderer or an infant."

2. In the case of punishment or retaliation, marriage and divorce ratification of the award by the Kazi is necessary.

*The Muslim Criminal Law**

According to the Muslim Jurisprudence the crime is defined as the violation of primary public (and private) rights. The wrong is called Mâa'si'at. It gives rise to certain "substitutory remedies" in the form of punishments, Uq'bât.[1]

The Muslim Law of Crimes falls under two distinct groups.

(1) Offences against God.

(2) Offences against private individuals.

The offences against God correspond to offences against the public, in other words all rights of God are public rights. In fact there are only two divisions of rights under the Muslim Law. The rights of God, *Huquq-Allah*, and rights of men *Huquq-ul 'Abad*. The obvious distinction between them is that the enforcement of the right of God is the duty of the State, while it is at the option of the person whose private right has been enfringed, to seek for its enforcement or pardon the wrongdoer[2].

---

*I omit the Muslim Civil Law as it is too lengthy to be discussed in these pages.

1. Blackstone defined crime, " as an act committed or omitted in violation of a public law forbidding or commanding it " (commentaries on the Laws of England). The Criminal law has its historical basis in the Law of revenge. In fact the maxim, " a tooth for a tooth, an eye for an eye, life for a life," though appears to be a crude formula for the administration of justice, marked a distinct step towards the progress of the Law of Crimes. The view that a crime is an offence against the state is a modern idea.

2. The classification of private rights is as follows:—

(a) Right to safety of person (nafs), (b) right to reputation (hurmat,) (c) rights of ownership (milk), (d) family rights, (*i*) Marital rights (zaujia), (*ii*) rights of guardianship (wilâyat), (*iii*) rights of children and poor relatives, (*iv*) right to succession (khilafat) and inheritance (wirasat). (e) right to do lawful acts (tasarrufât), (f) rights ex-contractu."
Abdur Rahim, Muhammadan Jurisprudence, p. 206.

Our jurists maintain the following classification.

(*a*) " Matters which are purely the right of God, that is public rights."

(*b*) " Matters which are entirely the right of individual men, that is private rights."

(*c*) " Matters in which public and private rights are combined but where the former preponderate."

(*d*) " Matters in which public and private rights are combined but where the latter preponderate."

The Muslim jurists classify punishment under three sub-divisions, (I) *Hadd*, (II) *Tazir*, (III) *Qisas*.

In law *Hadd*[1] means, " the correction appointed and specified by the law on account of the right of God." Its object is to deter and warn people, from the commission of such actions which are penalised by *Hadd*. *Hadd* is inflicted in the same manner both on the Muslims and non-Muslims. *Hadd* is liable in the following cases.

1. (*a*) Zinna, whoredom.[2]

(*i*) A married person convicted of whoredom is to be stoned.

(*ii*) an unmarried person is to be scourged with one hundred stripes.

(*iii*) A slave is to be given fifty stripes

2. *Hadd-Shirab* punishment for wine drinking[3]

(*i*) for free person eighty stripes,

(*ii*) for a slave forty stripes.

---

1. The Muslim Law of *Hadd* resembles the Hebrew Penal Law.

2. The doctrine of *Shuba* (error, doubt) plays an important part in dropping as a consequence the punishment of *Hadd* for instance in case " of doubt in the woman " there is no *hadd*. Similarly if whoredom was committed upon compulsion by the sovereign there is no punishment. The Muslim Law of Marriage by the present author, p. 14.

3. Punishment is not to be inflicted while the person remains in the state of intoxication.

3. *Hadd-Kazaf*, punishment for slander for accusing married persons of whoredom.

(*i*) for free person 80 stripes.
(*ii*) for a slave 40 stripes.

4. The punishment for apostasy is death.

Larcerny, Sarka.

5. *Sarka* means, secretly taking away of anothers property from lawful custody. Highway robbery is considered as "secretly taking away with respect to the Imâm whose duty it is to guard the highways."[1] According to the Hanafi law the value of a theft to incur punishment must be at least 10 dirhams [2]. The penalty prescribed is the cutting off the right hand of the thief. The free persons and slaves are to receive the same punishment. No distinction is made between them. Amputation is not incurred for stealing, "the use of which is allowed among Muslims or things which quickly decay, or a Koran or door of a mosque, or a free born person or an adult slave" [3] There is no amputation from stealing from a father or mother or child or from any prohibited relations, or from wife or husband. After amputation the property stolen is to be restored to the owner, but if it be lost or expended the thief is held no more to be responsible for it.

The highway robbery is classified under four divisions.

(1) Those thieves who are seized before they have committed robbery, for them the prescribed punishment is imprisonment until they repent.

(2) Those thieves who are seized after having committed robbery, the prescribed punishment for them is to cut off their right hand and left foot.

(3) Those thieves who are seized after having committed murder without robbery, (4) or with rob-

1. C. Hamilton, Hedaya Book, VIII, Ch. 1, p. 83.

2. According to Von Kremer a dirham is equivalent to the French france.

3. C. Hamilton, Hedaya Book, VIII, Ch. 1, pp. 89-91.

bery. The prescribed punishment for them is to put them to death. As regards the fourth case the punishment is to put them to death by means of amputation or crucify them.

The tendency of the Muslim law is not to inflict the punishment of Hadd as far as possible, with a view to attain this object they have made the laws of evidence strict to be complied with. For instance evidence of four male eye-witnesses is required to prove an instance of whoredom, and as such an act is committed in secret, it is usually impossible to prove even an actual instance. At the same time the witnesses deter in giving evidence, because of the law of slander, which makes them liable to receive 80 stripes for falsely accusing the persons. Similarly the Muslim law of theft was gradually modified. We can gather the penal law of theft at the time of Aurangzib from the Fatawa Alamgiri, and the firman issued by the Emperor to the diwan of Gujrat in 1672. Here are some of the instructions.[1]

"When theft is rife in the town and a thief is captured, do not even after proof behead him nor impale him as it may be his first offence. If a man has committed theft only once either less than or only up to the amount of the *nisab*....then chastise (*tazir*) him. But if he repeats the offence then after *tazir* keep him in prison till he repents. If he is not cured by *tazir* and imprisonment, but commits theft again, then sentence him to long term imprisonment or *siasat* and execution, and restore the stolen property to the owner, after legal proof of ownership if he be present. Otherwise deposit the property in trust (amanat) in the Bait-ul-mal."

"If an arrested thief speaks of his booty as lodged with another man, and it is discovered there, and the man is on investigation proved to be an accomplice of the thief—then, in the case of this being the first offence of the accomplice *tazir* him, but if it be habitual with him then after *tazir* imprison him till he reforms. But if these do not reform him and he commits the offence again, keep him permanently in prison."

1. J. N. Sarkar, Mughal Administration, p. 123.

II. *Tazir* in its literal sense means prohibition, in Law it means punishment decreed by the Shera either on account of the right of God or of the individual. In other words it is a discretionary punishment[1] in all cases for which *hadd* has not been fixed. It is of four kinds.

(*i*) " Chastisement proper to the most noble of the noble," mere admonition.

(*ii*) *Jirr*, dragging the offender out and exposing him to scorn.

(*iii*) imprisonment.

(*iv*) by blows, scourging

According to Imam Abu Hanifa and Muhammad the minimum number of stripes is three and the maximum is thirty nine, but Abu Yasuf held that the greatest number is seventy five stripes.

According to Abu Yusuf the fine is a " lawful chastisement in property ", but Hedaya rejects this doctrine. The Emperor Aurangzib apparently upheld, the view of the Hedaya. In the *firman* issued by him to the diwan of Gujrat he noted that, that all *amals* civil officers, found guilty should be imprisoned or dismissed or banished, but not punished with fine inasmuch as the Canon Law, does not recognise the penalty of fine[2].

In short the doctrine of *Tâ'zir* gives a wide latitude to the judge in inflicing punishment, and the entire system of the Muhammadan Criminal Law, as-siasat ushshara'ia, is based upon it. For instance we find that under special circumstances *Tazir* was being substituted even for *hadd*, in fact all new offences known to the Muslim Law in the progress of its

---

1. Abdur Rahim Muhammadan Jurisprudence, p. 362 " the range of this form of punishment extends from mere warning to fines corporal chastisement, imprisonment and transportation."

2. Ali Muhammad Khan Mirat-i-Ahmadi, J. N. Sarkar, Mughal Administration, p. 120.

development were dealt under the general head *Tâ'zir*. During the time of Aurangzib we had the following offences subject to *tazir*.[1]

" A counterfeit-coiner for the first time should be released after *tazir* and reprimand (*tahdid*); but if it be his profession then *tazir* and imprison him till he repents. But if he does not give up the practice detain him in long *captivity*."

" If a man buys false coins from a counterfeiter and utters them as good money same punishment as *above* except long imprisonment."

" If a man deceitfully administers poison to another, with fatal effect *tazir* and imprison him till he repents."

" For gambling with dice, *tazir* and confinement are the punishment. For repetition long imprisonment. Property won to be restored to owner or kept in trust."

The vendors of *bhang*, *buza* and similar intoxicants should be chastised and if habitual offenders, kept in prison till they repent."

III. Qisas, Retaliation, was sanctioned by immemorial customs in ancient Arabia. The law of compensation, diat, was also prevalent before the promulgation of Islam. The general theory is based upon the view that retaliation is a violation of the right of the public as well as private right, where the latter preponderates. Retaliation consists of the infliction by the injured person or by the deceased's heirs of similar injury or death upon the wrongdoer. Here we find the application of the broad maxim of the Mosaic Law, " a hand for a hand, an eye for an eye, a tooth for a tooth and the like." Retaliation being the right of the private person or his heirs, the law allows that the offence may be compounded on payment of compensation, and it may also be pardoned. In certain cases the offender's tribe, *Akilas*, is called upon to pay the blood money to the heirs of the deceased.

Under the Hanafi Law a Muslim or a non-Muslim, a free person or a slave all are considered on equal footing. It

1. J. N. Sarkar, Mughal Administration, p. 126.

is striking that the ancient Law considers offences against human life and body for instance murder as "more of an offence against the individual than the state," however in the Muslim countries the modern view is that offences against human life and body are no longer to be treated as "torts," but are to be punished as crimes and as offences against the public and the state. The Muslim Law discourages the application of the law of retaliation in all its rigidity, in fact retaliation as a remedy is unknown in actual practice in the greater part of the Muslim world.

According to the strict theory of the Muhammadan Law, the supreme ruler (Khalifa or Sultan) was liable to be punished for any offence committed by him, but later on this view was modified and the Hedaya states the cautious view. "If a supreme ruler (such as the *Khalif* for the time being) commit any offence punishable by Law, such as *whoredom, theft or drunkenness*, he is not subject to any punishment (but yet if he commit murder he is subject to the Law of retaliation and he is also accountable in matters of property) —because punishment is a right of God, the infliction of which is committed to the *Khalif* [or other Supreme Magistrate] and to none else, and he cannot inflict punishment upon himself as in this there is no advantage, because the good proposed in punishment is that it may operate as a warning to deter mankind from sin, and this is not obtained by a person inflicting punishment upon himself: contrary to the rights of the individual such as the laws of retaliation and of property, the penalties of which may be exacted of the *Khalif* as the claimant of right may obtain satisfaction either by the *Khalif* empowering him to exact his right from himself, or by the claimant appealing for assistance to the collective body of the Mussulman.[1]"

---

1. C. Hamilton Hedaya, (Grady), p. 188.

The Muslim Law of Evidence.

Under the Muhammadan Law it is obligatory upon witnesses when they are summoned to bear testimony.

The evidence required by the Muslim Law in criminal cases, is of two men but in the case of whoredom is of four men. The testimony of women is not admissible in all cases of punishment and retaliation. In all other cases, for instance marriage divorce agency and as regards property the evidence required is that of two men, or of one man and two women. According to Imam Shafi'i the evidence of woman is admissible in cases relating to property (e. g., hire, bail) only. However in certain cases which do not admit of the inspection of men the evidence of one woman is deemed sufficient, e. g., proof as to viginity and child birth. According to Imam Shafi'i four women are required in such cases. According to the Hanafi Law, the evidence of a blind man is inadmissible, but Imam Shafi'i holds that a blind man's evidence is admissible in matters where hearsay prevails. The evidence of a slave or of a slanderer is not admissible. The evidence in favour of a son or grandson or in favour of a father or grandfather or of a husband concerning his wife and vice versa, or of a master in favour of his slave or of a partner in favour of another partner, in matters relating to partnership property is inadmissible. Further according to the Hanafi Law the testimony is not admissible of atrocious criminals, nor of immodest persons, nor of usurers, nor of drunkards, nor of falconers, nor of public mourners and singers.

According to the juristic theory there are three kinds of evidence. The best form of oral testimony is known as *tawatur*, universal testimony, e. g., a large body of men accurately depose to the same facts. The second kind is called *Ahad*, a single or isolated testimony. This is an instance when the testimony is not universal. The third kind is called *Iqrar* an admission. The direct testimony is of highly probative value, that is there must be eye-witnesses but in certain cases hearsay evidence is admissible, e.g., paternity, death and marriage provided that the information was received from men of reliable character.

Circumstantial evidence, *Qarina'*, is also admissible provided it is, *Qatiatun*, of conclusive nature. Documentary evidence is also accepted for instance official documents and records of a Court of Justice can be tendered in evidence. There is also a kind of estoppel in the Muslim Law. The Law does not allow evidence to be given in respect of certain point having regard to the previous conduct of the parties. This is called *bayanud daruarat*, for instance if a certain person sells an article in the presence of the owner who keeps quiet. Then the owner's subsequent assertion that the person was not authorised to sell will be barred by this rule of estoppel.

If the witnesses retract their testimony before the judgment is delivered, such testimony will be rejected, but if afterwards it will not affect the Court's order. In the latter case the witnesses will be held liable if their evidence has caused miscarriage of justice.

Finally evidence repugnant to the claim cannot be admitted at all.

THE ADMINISTRATION OF JUSTICE OF MUSLIM LAW BY THE EAST INDIA COMPANY.

Immediately after the death of Emperor Aurangzib in A. D. 1707 the Mughal Empire lay in irretrievable ruin. It was natural for the system of administration of justice to fall along with the political power. The series of sovereigns that succeeded the great Emperor Alamgir exercised merely a nominal power in the districts round about the Capital. It was at this time that the Mahrattas, the French and the English represented by the East India Company, all had adopted an aggressive policy of annexation and rapid conquest. By the middle of the 18th century the Company began to combine with the ordinary mercantile pursuits, military and political activities. In 1757 after the battle of Plassey the supremacy of the Company was firmly established in Bengal.

The notable incident conferring legislative authority upon the Company occurred on the 12th of August A.D. 1765, when Lord Clive obtained the grant of the Diwani from the Mughal Emperor Shah Alum.[1] This act is generally considered as the assumption of sovereignty by the East India Company. The office of Diwan implied the collection of the provincial revenue and the administration of civil justice. The administration of Criminal Justice was conferred upon the Nawab Najm-ul-daulah and the Nawab received for the

---

1. The early legislative authority of the Company is found in the charter of Queen Elizabeth granted in A.D. 1601. Charters were granted by James I in A.D. 1609 and by Charles II in A.D. 1661 The charter of William III granted in A. D. 1698 established the foundation of the United Company subsequently designated the East India Company. Georges I's charter of 1726, established the famous Mayor's Courts and invested the Governors and Councils of the three Presidencies with power "to make, constitute. and ordain bye laws, rules, and ordinances for the good Government and regulation of the several corporations hereby created and of the inhabitants of the several towns, places and factories aforesaid respectively, and to impose reasonable pain and penalties upon all persons offending against the same or any of them." The charter of 1753 conferred similar powers (26 Geo. II).

maintenance of Nizamat a fixed stipend of fifty three laks of rupees.

Justice

The systems for the administration of Justice adopted by the Company are mainly based upon the regulations passed in the three Presidencies The plan adopted in Bengal being the foundation of the systems adopted in Bombay and Madras.[2]

Civil Justice in Bengal.

The Diwani was conferred on the East India Company by the firman of the 12th of August, 1765. The Indian officers carried on the general administration under the supervision of the English Rresident at the court of the Nawab till the year 1772, when the, court of Directors announced their intention " to stand forth as Diwan and by the agency of the Company's servants to take upon themselves the entire care and management of the revenues" [3] Warren Hastings and his coadjutors submitted a report which was adopted. The Exchequer and the Treasury were removed from Murshidabad to Calcutta. The Mufussil Diwani Adawluts known as the Provincial Civil Courts for the administration of civil justice were created. These courts were presided by the collectors in the capacity of Kings Diwans.[4] The courts took cognizance of all civil disputes.

1. The text of the firman was (Aitchison's Treaties India p, 60) "At this happy time our royal Firmaund. indispensably requiring obedience, is issued, that, whereas. in consideration of the attachment and services of the high and mighty.....the English Company we have granted them the Dewanny of the Provinces of Bengal, Behar and Orissa......as a free gift ....As the said Company are obliged to keep up a large army......We have granted to them whatsoever may remain out of the revenues of the said provinces, after remitting the sum of 26 lakhs of rupees to the royal Circar and providing for the expenses of the Nizamut.. .....Written the 24th of Sophar of the 6th year of the Jallos the 12th of August 1765.

2. In Bombay the Sadder and Mufussil Courts were established by A. D. 1799 and at Madras by A. D. 1802.

3 Fifth Report of the Select Committee of the House of Commons 1812 p. 5

4. In 1774 the European collectors were replaced by the Aamils.

The Hindus and Muhammadans were entitled to the benefit of their own laws, in all suits regarding inheritance and marriage.

The Sudder Diwani Adawlut at Calcutta was presided for sometime by the Governor-General, later by the famous judge Sir Elijah Impey. In 1780 the Chief Justice of the Supreme Court [1], who was appointed Judge of the Sudder Diwani Adawlut prepared various regulations which were incorporated in the code of 1781. In the same year the Sudder Diwani Adawlut was constituted by Act of Parliament (21 Geo. 111 c. 50 s 71) as a Court of Record.

In 1793 Lord Cornwallis established a regular gradation of Courts of Appeal. There were four Provincial Courts of Appeal [2]. These were presided by three European judges and had a Kazi, a Mufti and a Pandit to advise them. The appeals went from the Provincial Courts to the Sudder Diwani Adawlut at Calcutta [3]

During this period the Muhammadan law was undergoing a complete change. It ceased to be the national municipal law.

---

1. The Supreme Court of Calcutta was established by a Royal Charter in 1774. This court administered justice for the period of 88 years. The relation of the Court with the Supreme Council were unfortunately not happy. It also came into conflict with the Courts administering criminal justice. The famous trial and conviction of Nuncoomar, and the case of the Raja of Casigarh excited much attention. Consequently the Act of 1781. (21 Geo 111 c 70) was passed to set limits to the jurisdiction of the Supreme Court. The Supreme Court was abolished in 1860-62.

2. At Patna, at Dacca, at Murshidabad and one in the vicinity of Calcutta these courts were abolished in 1803.

3. The court at first consisted of the Governor-General and members of the Supreme Council. In 1801 it was made to consist of 3 judges and in 1811 it was made to consist of a chief judge and as many Puisne judges as the Governor General in Council may appoint (Reg. XII 1811 s. 2). In 1797 by Reg XVI provision was made for the conduct of appeals from the Sudder Diwani to the King in Council.

Criminal Justice in Bengal.

According to the firman of 1765, the Nizamut or administration of criminal justice was left under the supervision and control of the Nawab. The Muhammadan Courts were retained and "The Muhammadan law was in force throughout the country." [1]. The old officers were still retained. The Nawab himself tried all capital cases. The faujdar and Nawab's deputies tried all cases of quarrels and frays etc. The Muhtasib as usual tried all cases of drunkenness and sel ing liquors. The Kutwal was still the prefect of the Police.

In A. D 1772 Warren Hastings completely transformed the machinery for the administration of criminal justice The office of Nawab Diwan was abolished, the work was taken up by the British Agency A new court of criminal Judicature called the Faujdary Adawlut was established in each district for the trial of "murder, robbery and theft, and all other felonies, forgery, perjury, and all sorts of frauds and misdemeanours, assaults, frays, quarrels, adultery, and every other breach of the peace or violent invasion of property" [2]. In these criminal courts the Kazi or Mufti with the assistance of two Maulvies sat to hold trials ? The English Collectors of Revenue were however directed to superintend the proceedings of these courts. These Faujdary Adawluts were under the control of the Sudder Nizamut Adawlat established at Murshidabad. This supreme court was presided by a Darugha as the chief officer, who was appointed by the Nazim. The Chief Kazi, Kazi-ul-Kuzat and the Chief Mufti and three Maulvis sat to assist the Darugha in discharging his duties. The duty of the court was "to revise all the proceedings of the Faujdary adawluts and in capital cases, by signifying their approbation and disapprobation thereof, with their reasons at large, to prepare the sentence for the warrant of the Nazim" [2]. This court, shortly after its inauguration, was removed

1. H. Cowell Courts and Legislative authorities p. 27.

2. Plan Rule VII W. H. Morley, An Analytical Digest p. XXXV

to Calcutta, but in A D. 1775 it was removed back to Murshidabad where it discharged its duties under the control of the Nazim for fifteen years. The Muhammadan law as modified by various regulations was administered in the courts. In 1790 by Lord Cornwallis' regulations the powers of the Nazim were transferred to the Governor General in Council, and the entire system of the administration of criminal justice was remodelled.

At Calcutta the Nizamut Adawlut consisted of the Governor-General and members of the Supreme Council assisted by the Kazi-ul-kuzat and two muftis.[2] This court was the court of Criminal Appeal and also a Board of Police. Four courts of circuit consisting of two judges assisted by Kazis and Muftis as assessors[3] were also established, and in capital cases they were to report their decisions for the confirmation of the Nizamut Adawlut at Calcutta. The Judicial Regulation XXVI 1790 S. 33 provided that in trials for murder the doctrine of Abu Yusuf and Muhammad requiring the evidence of criminal intention was to be applied in giving Fatwa of the Law officers. By Jud. Reg. XXVI the relations of a murdered person were debarred from pardoning the offender. In 1791 the Judges of the courts of circuit wherever they dissented from the Fatwa of the law officers were required to refer the case to the Nizamut Adawlut.

By Jud. Reg. XXXIII 1791 S. 3 imprisonment and hard labour was substituted for mutilation, and the Nizamut Adawlut wss required to pass the sentence of death instead of granting "Diyat" to the heir. By Reg. II 1801 S. 10 the constitution of the Nizamut Adawlut was altered, instead of the Governor-General and council the court consisted of

---

1. Warren Hastings presided in the Chief Criminal Court at Calcutta for about eleven months. At Mursidabad the Nizamat Adawlut was under the supervision of Muhammad Riza Khan.

2. Jud. Reg. XXVI 1790 Preamble.

3. W. H. Morley An Analytical Digest Vol. 1 p. XLIII.

three judges [1] assisted by the Chief Kazi of Bengal, Bihar, Orissa and Benares [2] and two Muftis.

In 1829 the courts of circuit were abolished and commissioners of circuit were appointed with the same powers as judges of circuit. Gradually the practice grew up of appointing "District and Sessions Judges."

A High Court was established at Calcutta by the charters in 1862–1865. The High Court took up the administration of Justice of the Civil and Criminal Law. The court of the Sudder Nizamut (Faujdary Adawlut) was abolished.

In 1802 the Madras Government founded a system for the administration of Justice, there were the Native Commissioners, and the zillah courts and the Provincial Courts (four in number) were to hear appeals from the zillah courts. The plan for the administration of criminal justice was the same as in Bengal The Faujdary Adawlut was the chief criminal court. It consisted of the Governor and members of the council 'All these criminal courts administered the Muhammadan Law as modified by the Regulations."[3]

Madras.

Thus the Muhammadan Criminal Law was administered in the Madras Presidency and the usual fatawas were given in each case, however Act I of 1840 dispensed altogether with the Fatwa, but it still retained the principles of the Muhammadan Law. The Madras High Court was established by the charters in 1862—1865. The High Court exercises both civil and criminal jurisdiction.

---

1. Reg XII 1811 S. 2 increased the number of Judges as in the Sudder Diwani Adawlut.

2. Reg. IX of 1793 sec. 67 Reg XXXIX of 1793 and Reg. XLIX of 1795 extended the Kazis jurisdiction to Benares but Reg. VIII of 1809 provided for the abolition of the office of Kazi.

3. W. H. Morley's Analytical Digest Vol. 1 p. LXIV.

In Western India the predecessor of the English were the Marathas, consequently, there was no trace of the Muhammadan Law either Civil or Criminal in that province. In 1797 the Bombay Government was authorised to constitute courts of civil and criminal Judicature on the system introduced by Lord Cornwallis, in Bengal. Tthe Muhammadan Criminal Law did not generally prevail. The Hindus were tried by the Hindu Criminal Law, the Parsis and Christians by the English Law.[1] Thus in the development of the judicial system in the Bombay Presidency the Muhammadan Law was of no importance. The Bombay High Court was established by charters in 1862-65. The High Court exercises both civil and criminal Jurisdiction.

Bombay.

In Benares a Court of Justice was established in 1781 and similar courts were established at Jaunpur, Mirzapur and Ghazipur in 1788. These courts administered the Muhammadan Law.[2] By Reg. VI of 1831 a Sudder Diwani Adawlut was established in the North Western Provinces on the same system as was prevalent in Bengal. In 1866 the High Court was established at Allahabad, it exercises both civil and criminal jurisdiction.

N. W. Provinces.

The Punjab was the first to be conquered by the Muslims and the Muslim law was administered there till the rise of the Sikh power. In A. D. 1849 the Punjab became a British Province The Governor-General instead of introducing the Bengal system of the administration of justice gave a general instruction to uphold native institutions and practices so far as they are consistent with the distribution of justice to all classes.

The Punjab.

---

1. Reg. V 1799 S. 36 and Reg. III 18000 S. 36.
2. Archibold W. A. J. Indian Constitutional History, p. 140.

We have surveyed briefly the civil and criminal administration of Justice by the East India Company. We have seen that in the civil courts and especially in the criminal courts the Muhammadan law was being administered and the Muhammadan officers of justice were retained. In Warren Hasting's plan for the establishment of judicial system it was distinctly provided that the "Maulavis" were to attend the courts and expound the Muhammadan law.

The progress of the Muslim law.

The following procedure is suggested from the letter of the Committee of Circuit to the Council at Fort William, dated Cassimbazar, August 15, 1772:—[1]

"The Cazee is assisted by the Muftee and Mohtassib in this court. After hearing the parties and evidences, the Muftee writes the Fettwa or the law applicable to the case in question, and the Cazee pronounces judgment accordingly. If either the Cazee or Mohtassib disapprove of the Fettwa, the case is referred to the Nazim, who summons the Ijlass or General Assembly, consisting of the Cazee, Mufti, Mohtassib, the Darogas of the Adawlut, the Maulavis and all learned in the law, to meet and decide upon it. Their decision is final."

In the Civil matters the Muhammadan Law was easily superseded, but it continued for a long time to be administered in the criminal courts. However it was not the pure Muhammadan Law.[2] It was being modified by various regulations, and the Muhammadan tribunals administered the Muslim law subject to the supervision of an English authority. Morley[3] suggests that the Government assumed itself to possess an inherent right to alter the provision of the Muhammadan Law, and this appears to have been tacitly

1, Archbold W. A .J Indian Constitutional History, page 51.

2. The regulation of 1772, section 72 "in all suits regarding inheritance succession, marriage and caste and other religious institutions or usages the laws of the Koran with respect to Muhammadans.............shall invariably be adhered to"

3. W. H. Morley. "An Analytical Digest", p. CLXXVI.

upheld by the Parliament (13th Geo. III C. 63 S 7). The President and Council frequently interposed and altered the Law Nevertheless the Government was extremely reluctant to interfere with the application of Muhammadan Criminal law. The following letter addressed by the Collector of Islamabad to the Officer Commanding, the Company's troops at Chittagong, strinkingly illustrates this view :—[1]

"Sir,

"Agreeable to a *derkaste* (application) delivered to me by Muhammad Summee, Darogah of the Nizamat Adawlut, I have to request you will grant him a party sufficiently strong to assist him in carrying into execution the Fetwahs of the Nazim upon Mahommed Shuffee, Mahommed Rustum, Ameer Mahommed and Loodie Dacoits, who are to suffer Impaiement and I beg leave to acquaint you that for the sake of example the Darogah proposes to have the sentences executed in four different divisions of the province, viz at the Funny Soorporah, Muriascrai and Jugecollah.

I am, Sir,

Your most obedient humble servant,

John Buller

Islamabad, the 12th October, 1781.

Here is a letter from Warren Hastings[1] :—

"The officers of the Nizamat have again declared the propriety of the sentence, and that is strictly conformable to the Muhammedan Law. As the natives are not to be tried according to our notions of justice, but by the law of the country, *excepting in very extraordinary cases where it has been usual for Government to interpose*, I must request that you will permit the officers appointed for that purpose to carry the enclosed warrant into immediate execution.

I am, Sir,

Your most obedient humble servant,

Warren Hastings."

---

1. Roland Wilson Digest of Anglo-Muhammadan Law, page 30

The italics is in Hastings' own hand-writing.

In 1790 the abolition of the office of Nawab Nazim weakened the position of the Muhammadan tribunals, but the criminal courts were directed to administer the Muhammadan Law, and in cases of murder the sentence was to be according to the opinions of Imam Abu Yusuf and Imam Muhammad[1]. The same was the direction to the criminal courts established in 1793.[2]

The administration of justice of the Muslim Law was further weakened by the abolition of the office of Kazi in 1809[3] from the Nizamat Adawlut, and in 1832 it was enacted in Bengal that all persons, who where not Muhammadans, might claim to be exempted from the trial under the Muhammadan criminal law for offences cognizable under the general regulations.[4]

The Act XI of 1864 abolished the offices of Muhammadan Law officers, the Kazi-ul-kuzat and of subordinate Kazis,[5] however in 1880 the Kazis' Act XII[6] was passed which gave

---

1. Beng. Reg. XXVI 1790, Ss. 32, 33.

2. Beng. Reg IX 1793, Ss. 47, 50, 74, 75.

3. Reg. VIII of 1809.

4. Beng. Reg VI 1832, S. 5

5. "An Act to repeal the laws relating to the offices of Hindoo and Muhammadan Law officers and to the offices of Cazi-ul-cozaat and of Kazi, and to abolish the former officers (Repealed by Act VIII of 1868).

6. Act XII of 1880, Section 4.

"Nothing herein contained and no appointment made hereunder shall be deemed—

(a) To confer any judicial or administrative powers or any Kazi or Naib Kazi appointed hereunder · or

(b) To render the presence of a Kazi or Naib Kazi necessary at the celebration of any marriage or the performance of any rite or ceremony ; or

(c) To prevent any person discharging any of the functions of a Kazi.

power to the Local Government to appoint Kazis in any local area after consulting the principal Muhammadan residents of such local area. These Kazis possess no judicial or administrative powers, the only function which they now usually perform is to help in the celebration of marriage, and even here their presence is not essential. The Regulations were thus the instruments which gradually abolished the Muhammadan Law. The change was very gradual, it was hardly perceptible by the people.

Immediately after the Proclamation of the Queen, in 1858 the Civil Procedure Code[1], the Penal Code[2] and the Criminal Procedure Code, all of which have been in preparation for a long time were enacted. These three Codes were passed respectively in 1859, 1860, and 1861, and in 1861 the Indian High Courts Act 24 and 25 Vic. C 104 authorised the Queen to establish the High Courts in Calcutta, Madras and Bombay. The Allahabad High Court was established in 1866. The result of passing these measures was to establish in India a uniform Law and a uniform system of Civil and Criminal Courts. The Indian Penal Code has completely superseded the Muhammadan Criminal Law.

Sir Roland Wilson says : "The system was gradually Anglicised by successive Regulations, the Muhammadan element did not entirely disappear till 1862, when the Penal Code and the first Code of Criminal Procedure came into force, nor as regards rules of evidence till the passing of the Indian Evidence Act in 1872"[1] The modifications resulting in the pure Muhammadan Law, "from British manipulation" are of supreme importance Act V of

---

1. At present we have the Civil Procedure Code Act V of 1908.

2. The Indian Penal Act XLV of 1860 and the Criminal Procedure Code Act V of 1898, as amended by the Acts of 1923.

3. The High Courts Act 1911, 1 & 2 Geo. V. C. 18.

4. Anglo-Muhammedan Law, p. 30.

1843 abolished slavery throughout the British India with the result the Muhammadan Law of slavery was made inoperative. Similarly Act XXI of 1850 abolished the civil disabilities which the Muhammadan Law attached to apostasy by enacting that the right of inheritance shall not be lost by renouncing any religion. The Indian Majority Act of 1875 has also affected the provisions of the Muhammadan Law. Lastly by enacting the Waqf Validating Act of 1913 the Government has interposed to respect the integrity of the pure Muhammadan Law which was being assailed by the judiciary. The Waqf Act of 1923 is another monumental enactment, for the better management of the Waqf property, in conformity with the laws of Islam.

The following few cases will illustrate the administration of Justice of Muslim Criminal law by the Courts of the East India Company :—[1]

Administering Poisonous or deleterious Drugs.

Administering a deleterious drugs (dhatura), to the effects of which the death of the deceased is to be attributed, not coming within the five fold definition of culpable homicide under the Muhammedan Law, the prisoner was declared liable to discretionary punishment by Akubat and imprisoned for life. Government V. Mt. Sookhoo, 29th July 1800, I.N. A. Rep. 216 Harington & Fombelle.

The Fatwa declared that the act of giving poison with a murderous intent to one person, by means of which poison a third person is unintentionally killed, is not, by Muhammadan Law, punishable with death. But the Nizamat Adawlut may inflict capital punishment under the provision of Cl. 1 Sec. 10 of Reg. VIII of 1803......Sentence, death. Government V Mt. Indeea, 20th Dec. 1813. 1 N.A. Rep. 287 —Fombelle 8 Rees.

---

1. W. H. Morley, Analytical Digest, p. 115.

Affray.

"The Muhammadan Law makes a distinction between him who is proved to have struck the deceased in an affray, and those present aiding and abetting. The Nizamut Adawlut considered all present equally culpable, and sentenced them accordingly to imprisonment for five years."

Mt. Soondree *v.* Bojoo Gaynee and others, 30th April, 1814, I N. A. Rep. 299—Colebrook & Fombelle."

Burglary.

"If a thief breaks through the wall of a house and entering therein take the property of another, and deliver it to an accomplice standing at the entrance of the breach, the specific penalty of Hadd prescribed by the Muhammadan Law for larceny without violence (Sarakah-i-Sogra) is not incurred by either of the parties. Sentence twenty-five korahs and imprisonment in banishment for fourteen years, Poorun *v.* Munghraw and another, 6th February, 1813, I N. A. Rep. 255—Fombelle & Rees."

Compulsion, Homicide by.

"The prisoner having killed the deceased by order of his master, and under fear of immediate death in case of refusal, the *Fatwas* declared that he was not liable to *Kisas* and should be released. The court accordingly directed his immediate release, Boodhun *v.* Ratra, 30th Jan., 1806, I N. A. Rep. 101—Harington & Fombelle."

False Personation.

"False personation for one's own advantage is an offence under the Muhammadan Law..........the punishment is at the discretion of the Hakim ......" Government *v.* Aluk Shah, 13th June, 1839, 5 N. A. Rep. 122—Bradden & Tucker."

Murder.

"A boy aged fourteen years was convicted of the murder of a boy of eleven years of age for his ornaments. The Fatwa declared Kisas barred as the prisoner had not attained the age of puberty and that he was liable to discretionary punishment by Tazir. Sentence, imprisonment in transportation for life. Poorun *v.* Budlooah, 11th June, 1810, I N. A. Rep. 213—Stuart."

"A woman and her son, a boy aged nine years were convicted by the Fatwa, the former of the murder of a child for its ornaments, and the latter of aiding in the same. The mother was sentenced to death, and the son, in consideration of his extreme youth, was discharged without punishment, under the discretion left by the Fatwa." Laljee *v.* Mt. Soobhanee and another, 21st July, 1807, I N. A. Rep. 152—H. Colebrooke & Fombelle."

Public Justice.

"The Muhammadan Law admits the right of the ruling power to punish serious offences for the ends of justice though the injured party waive his private claim." Mt. Sebha *v.* Moyunoola, 19th September, 1818, I N. A. Rep. 367—Harington & Fendall."

Trove.

"Under the Muhammadan Law a Multakit, or finder, failing to make public advertisement of Luktah or trove property, subjects himself to discretionary punishment, Chundoo *v.* Sheikh Roopun and others, 15th May, 1815, I N. A. Rep. 308—Fombelle and Ker."

The Privy Council and the High Courts.

The decisions of the Privy Council and the Indian High Courts have had considerable affect on the Muslim Law. In Khajah Husain Ali *v.* Shazadih Hazari Begum[1]. Markby. J. observed: "The means of discovering the Muhammadan Law which this court possesses are so extremely limited that I am glad to avail myself of any mode of escaping a decision on any point connected therewith." While in Mallick Abdool Gafoor *v.* Mulika.[2] Garth, C. J. observed: "In dealing with these points we must not forget that the Muhammadan Law, to which our attention has been directed in works of very ancient authority, was promulgated many centuries ago in Baghdad and other Muhammadan countries under a very different state of laws and society from that which now prevails in India and although we do our best here in suits between Muhammadans to follow the rules of Muhammadan Law, it is often difficult to discover what these rules really were.......... we must endeavour as far as we can to ascertain the true principles upon which

1. 12 Weekly Reporter, 344—7.
2. 10 Calcutta, 1123.

that law was founded, and to administer it with due regard to the rules of equity and good conscience, as well as to the laws and state of society and circumstances which now prevail in this country." However again in Aga Mahomed *v.* Kulsum Bibi [1] the court observed: "It would be wrong for the court on a point of this kind to put their own construction on the Quran in opposition to express ruling of commentators of such great antiquity and high authority." Thus the opinion expressed by the Bench is indecisive. But if the Privy Council and the Indian High Courts consider themselves (as they really are in fact) to have displaced the Muhammadan tribunals, Kazis and Muftis, then it is submitted, that the development of the Anglo-Muhammadan Law ought not to be hampered by any consideration, it is to be developed on the principle of equity and good conscience with due regard to the state of society and circumstances of the country. The principle of *Ijtihad* has been the avenue for the development of the Muslim Law, and that can always be applied to develop the Anglo-Muhammadan Law to suit the requirements of the time. Law is the product of the entire history of the people. It is an evolution by an organic growth.

1. 25 Calcutta, 9.

THE ZIMMIS UNDER THE ADMINISTRATION OF JUSTICE OF MUSLIM LAW.

When the Empire of Islam extended far and wide the non-Muslims, Zimmis, became the subjects of the conquerors. The Muslim rulers followed the principles established by the Prophet of Islam, which was one of absolute non-interference in religious matters, and guarantee of protection of life and property under the general laws of the land. The Prophet himself set the noblest example by treating the Muslims and non-Muslims equally in the eye of the law. Ta'ma bin Ubairaq stole a coat of mail and having hidden it at a Jew's place accused the Jew of the theft. Ta'ma was supported in this contention by his entire tribe. The Holy Prophet cleared the Jew of the charge,[1] notwithstanding the fact that verdict against Ta'ma would mean alienation of the entire tribe. On another occasion when the Jews of Khabayr were accused of the murder of Abdullah ibn Sahl the Prophet declined to decree qisas as no eye-witnesses were produced.

The following instructions were given by the first Khalifa Abu Bakr to the Muslim army on the eve of their departure to Persia.

"O, People stop remember these ten commands: (1) Don't misappropriate; (2) Don't deceive; (3) Don't disobey; (4) Don't mutilate anyone; (5) Don't kill old men, women and children; (6) Don't destroy or burn fruit

يا ايها الناس قفوا اوصيكم
بعشر فاحفظوا ها على—لاتخونوا
اولاتغلوا ولا تغدروا ولا تمثلوا ولا
تقتلوا طفلاً ولا شيخاً ولا كبيراً
ولا امراة ولا تعقروا نخلاً ولا
تحرقوه ولا تقطعوا الشجرة

1. This instance is said to be the occasion of the revelation of the important Koranic verse on Justice. part V. ch. IV. See Maulvi Muhammad Ali, The Holy Quran, p. 231.

and date trees, (7) Don't slaughter camel, cows and goats, except to relieve starvation; (8) You will meet such men who are devotees living in seclusion; leave them unmolested. (9) You will meet such men who will offer you food, when you partake of it, thank the Lord; (10) You will also meet such men who deserve chastisement. Now start in the name of God, may Lord protect you from all deseases and your enemies."

المثمرة ولا تذبحوا شاة ولا بقرة
ولا بعيراً الا لماكلة وسوف تمرون
باقوام قد فرغوا انفسهم بالصوامع
فدعوهم وما فرغوا انفسهم وسوف
تقدمون على قوم ياتوكم بانية
فيها الوان الطعام فاذا اكلتم منها
شيئاً بعد شئ فاذكروا اسم الله
عليها و تلقون اقواماً قد فحصوا
اوساط روسهم و تركوا حولها مثل
العصائب فاخفقوا هم بالسيف
خفقاً اندفعوا بإسم الله افناكم الله
الطعن والطاعون -

Treaty.

Here is the text of the treaty of Palestine which illustrates what rights were granted to the Christians and the Jews.

"This is the protection which the servant of God Amir-ul-Muminin grants to the people of Palestine. This protection is for their lives property, Church, Cross for the healthy and the sick and for all their co-religionists.

In this way that their churches shall not be turned into dwelling houses, nor will they be pulled down nor any injury will be done to them or to their enclosures, nor to their Cross and nor will anything be deducted

هذا ما اعطى عبدالله عمر امير
المومنين اهل ايليا من الامان
اعطاهم اماناً لانفسهم و اموالهم
و كنائسهم و صلبانهم و سقيمها
؛ بريها و سائر ملتها انه لا يسكن
كنائسهم ولا تهدم ولا ينتقص منها
ولا من حيزها ولا من صليبهم
ولا من شي من اموالهم ولا
يكرهون على دينهم ولا يضار احد
منهم ولا يسكن بايليا معهم احد
من اليهود و على اهل ايلياء
ان يعطوا الجزية كما يعطي اهل
المداين و عليهم ان يخرجوا منها
الروم و و اللصوت فمن خرج منهم

from their wealth. No restriction shall be made regarding their religious ceremonies no Jews will be allowed to stay along with them.

It shall be incumbent upon the people of Palestine, that they shall pay *Jazya* (the capitation tax) like other cities. They must expel the Greeks and those of them who shall leave the city shall be protected and conducted

فهو آمن و عليه مثل اهل الايلياء
من الجزية و من احب من اهل
ايلياء ان يسير بنفسه وماله مع الروم
و يخلي بيعهم و صليبهم حتي
يبلغوا مامنهم و علي ما في هذا
الكتاب عهد الله و ذمة رسوله و
ذمة الخلفاء و ذمة المومنين اذا
اعطوا الذي عليهم من الجزية شهد
علي ذلك خالد بن الوليد و عمر
و بن العاص - و عبدالرحمن بن
عوف و معاوية بن ابي سفيان
و كتب و حضر سنة ١٥ه.

safely to their destination but those of them who would prefer to remain in Palestine shall also receive, protection and they are to pay Jazya. And of the people of Palestine who would like to leave with the Greeks, then their Churches and Cross also shall be protected, and they may safely go to their destination. Whatever is in this document is guaranteed in the name of God and the Prophet by the Khalifa and the Faithful on condition that the people pay Jazya regularly. This document is witnessed by Khalid bin Walid Umar bin Al'as Abdur Rahman bin Awf and Muawiyah bin Abie Safiyan, dated A. H. 15."

The Khalifa Umar even considered that the poor and old Zimmis were legally entitled to receive protection from the Bait-ul-mal, and he issued a general order to the Head of the Treasury declaring that the order of God to distribute charity to the poor includes the followers of any revealed religion.[1] It is related the occasion when he issued this order was that he saw an old Jew begging in the street.

انظر هذا وضرباءه فوالله ما انصفناه ان اكلنا شبيبته ثم
نخذله عند الهرم انما الصدقات للفقراء والمساكين و الفقراء هم
المسلمون و هذا من المساكين من اهل الكتاب -

The Laws of the Land.

Of all the branches of the Muhammadan law, the law of evidence has placed a permanent disqualification on the non-Muslims. While the testimony of Zimmis with respect to each other is admissible, the Hanafi lawyers hold that their evidence concerning a Muslim is inadmissible.[1] Similarly it provides that the testimony of an infidel ***Mustamin***, with relation to a Zimmi is not admissible but the evidence of a Zimmi is admissible with respect to a ***Mustamin***. However the testimony of one ***Mustamin*** is admissible as regards another ***Mustamin*** provided they belong to the same country otherwise not.[2]

As regards the law of crimes and murder the Muslim law treated the Muslims and the non-Muslims equally and the cases decided by the Prophet and the Khulafa-ur-Rashidun and by the subsequent Khalifas illustrate this point fully. There is a well-known saying of Ali to the effect that the Zimmis are like ourselves, their blood is our blood.[3]

The Muslim law of crimes prescribes for the non-Muslims the same punishment of Hadd for fornication, adultery, theft, dacoity as it does for the Muslims.

During the reign of Umar Qabila Bakr bin Dail murdered a Christian. Umar on hearing it ordered Qabila to be handed over to the heirs of the deceased[4]. There were similar cases reported in the time of Usman Ali and Umar bin Abdul Aziz.[5]

As regards the law of the right of property and right of land the Muslim law treated the Muslims and the non-

---

1. The Shafi'i jurists hold that Zimmis of the same religion may depose for and against their co-religionists but not in case of Zimmis professing other religion.

2. C. Hamilton, Hedaya Vol. II, Book XXI, p 691.

3. من كان له ، متقتدمه كدمنا ، وديته كديتنا -

4. Risial Shibli (in Urdu), p. 48.

5. Ibid, p. 49.

Muslims equally. A non-Muslim was considered to be the owner of the land, and quiet possession was guaranteed by the laws of Islam. The lands were purchased from the Zimmis by the Khalifas if they acquired it for the state purposes. For instance the Khalifa Umar purchased a site for building a Mosque at Kufa[1]. The Abbaside Khalifa Munsur purchased the land where he founded the city of Baghdad[2].

Imam Abu Yusu expressed this view in the Kitab-ul Khiraj thus:

"The Khalifa for the time being has no right to deprive them (the Zimmis) of their lands. It is their property and is inheritable by their heirs."

كتاب الخراج

وليس له أن يا خذها بعد
ذالک منهم ، هی ملک لهم
يتوارثونهوا و يتبايعونها -

Umar I had ordained that the Muslims were not to acquire land or follow agricultural pursuits. Similarly Umar ibn Abdul Aziz enacted a law in A. H. 100 declaring that every puchase of land by a Muslim was null and void. This law continued till the time of Khalifa Hisham. Umar II had also ordained that the priests of tolerated religious institution should not sell their landed properties. If a Muslim was found to have purchased the land, he forfeited his purchase money to the Government and the land was restored to the Rayyat.[3] The incidental effect of this policy was that the non-Muslims continue to enjoy possession and ownerships of their landed property.

The tolerant spirit of Umar II was remarkable. The great mosque of Damascus was built near a church.

---

1. Fatuh-al-Baldan, p. 286.
2. Ibid 298.
3. S. Khuda Bukhsh, the Orient under the Caliphs, p. 209, on the authority of ibn Askir.

Muawiyah attempted to incorporate the church building in the mosque, but the Christians refused to surrender the sacred church. Abdul Malik also endeavoured to acquire the land, on payment, from the church authorities. Finally Walid compulsory acquired the church and incorporated it in the mosque. During the reign of Umar II the Christians made a representation to restore the church to them, and Umar II issued an order for the restoration of the enclosure, included in the mosque. The matter however, ended in a compromise by which the great mosque was saved from demolition and all the churches near Damascus were restored to the Christians.[1] On one occasion Umar II in the capacity of the Kazi decreed a suit in favour of a Christian against Khalifa Hisham.[2] Similarly the tolerant rule of the Abbaside Khalifas had revolutionised the entire country. The Jews by merits had attained to influential positions, and a contemporary poet observed : " The Jews of our time have reached the goal of their ambition. To them belong power and authority. Out of them are chosen counsellors and princes."[3] The non-Muslims who held responsible posts were Bakhtishiu Jibrii, Salamuya, Hanayn bin Ishaq, Yuhanna bin Masuya, Abu Ishaq Sabi and Sabit bin Qurrat.[4]

In the history of the Muslim Kingdoms there are instances where the non-Muslims were illegally treated, nay there are instances of brutal treatment, but the Islamic Shera is no way responsible for the ill-treatment of the non-Muslims. In fact the brutal incident of Kerbala, the occasion of the murder of the grandson of the Prophet fully illustrates that the Muslim Kings in their love for the aggrandisement of power and conquest did not even leave,

---

1. Fatuh-ul-baldan, p. 125.
2. Risail Stubhi, p. 62 on the authority of Aiun biihidaq.
3. S. Khuda Bukhsh 'the Orient under the Caliphs,' p. 225.
4. Risail Shibli, p. 67.

the immediate descendants of their own Prophet unmolested. If that was so, some of the instances of the treatment of the non-Muslims is better imaginable than described in these few pages.

Turkey.

Of the later Muslim Empires Turkey[1] came closely in contact with the non-Muslim population. In A. D. 1453 Muhammad II surnamed the Conqueror captured Constantinople. His entry into the capital of the Byzantine Empire is remarkable for his equitable treatment of the non-Muslim population. Muhammad granted extremely liberal privileges to the Zimmis, he established an almost independent rule of an essentially theocratic character within his own Government for the administration of Justice, and for the benefit of his non-Muslim subjects. Here is an account given by Davey, "He next exorted him in state to the gates of a palace which he had given to the Orthodox Church to be the Patriarchal residence for ever, and granted him privileges greater than any which had been enjoyed by his predecessors, under the Byzantine Emperors, for in addition to the full exercise of his spiritual authority, he was to consider himself the supreme temporal ruler of the Greek population, not in Constantinople only, but throughout the Empire, the other Archbishops and Bishops being subject to him. The Sultan gave him a body of Janissaries to wait upon him.........He annexed a Court of Justice to his Palace and handed his Beatitude the keys of a well appointed torture chamber and of a correspondingly awe inspiring prison."[2] Indeed the Greek Government under the Ottoman Sultans was purely theocratic, the "Kapu Kiaia"[3] served as itermediary between the Sultan and the Diwan. In the villages a Mayor was elected on the first Sunday after Easter

1. I do not propose to deal with the history of Capitulations and what events led to its abolition by the Turkish Government of Angora.

2. The Sultan and His subjects, Vol. I, p. 117.

3. Ibid, Vol. II, p. 109.

in each year. The Mayor selected magistrates and constituted a sort of non-ecclesiastical municipal council.

Similarly to the Armenians, the Sultan assigned a Patriarchal Palace and a prison. In 1415 when the Jews were driven out of Spain to escape the Inquisition, about 30,000 of them took refuge at Constantinople, the Sultan welcomed them, and placed them under the Chief Rabbi or Kat Kham Bachi to whom he granted similar judicial powers as the Greek Patriarch. The record of the Turkish administration of Justice with respect to the non-Muslims stands out pre-eminently. The history of the world does not furnish a similar instance of tolerance and good faith. The trouble with the Ottoman non-Muslim population really dates from A. D. 1720. When Peter the Great concluded a treaty placing Russia on equal footing with the other powers. By the Treaty of Belgrade 1739 and by subsequent development Russia eventually came in the position to assume the protectorate of the Ottoman Sultan's Orthodox subjects. This idea of protection was borrowed by the Ottoman Sultans, and it served a very useful purpose for asserting the rights of Khilafat in the non-Muslim states. For instance the Treaty of Kuchuk Kainarji of 1774 described the Sultan as the Khalifa, and as regards the Tartars who were to pass under the Russian control, the Treaty laid down that they " being of the same faith as the Musalmans, must, in regard to his Sultanic Majesty, as Supreme Caliph of the Mahomedan Law, conform to the regulations which their law prescribes to them...."

Similarly when in 1908 Austria annexed Bosnia and Herzegovina the Turkish Government entered into an agreement providing that the Sultan should continue to be recognised as the Khalifa, and his name should be mentioned in the public prayers, and that the Ra'is-ul-ulama, who controlled ecclesiastical affairs in Bosnia and Herzegovina, should continue to be subordinate to the Shiekh-ul-Islam of

Constantinople. The Treaty of Lausanne of 1912 between Turkey and Italy also provided that the Sultan's name is to mentioned in the Khutba and that the Chief Kazi of Libya is to be under the Sheikh-ul-Islam. The Treaty of Constantinople (1913) between Bulgaria and Turkey also provided that the Chief Mufti shall be elected by the Muftis of Bulgaria, and shall receive an investiture from the Sheikh-ul-Islam who should control the administration of Shera in Bulgaria. A similar agreement with certain modifications was entered between Turkey and Greece also. These instances embodied in the various treaties incidentally illustrate the application of the Shera of Islam in independent states.

The Dar-ul-Islam and Dar-ul-Harb.

The Shera of Islam has been wisely preserved as the general law applicable to the Muslims inhabiting outside the territorial limits of Islam. This brings us to a distinction maintained in the Muslim Law between the Dar-ul-Islam and Dar-ul-Harb. The country governed by a Muslim ruler is known as Dar-ul-Islam, literally territory of safety. The Dar-ul-Harb literally means the territory of war, and it is the appellation given to a country ruled by a non-Muslim power. According to Imam Abu Yusuf and Imam Muhammad a country is designated Dar-ul-Harb if the laws of non-Muslims only are promulgated there. But if in a particular country the Muslim Laws are enforced for the Muslims and non-Muslim Laws are enforced for the non-Muslims, that is to say both systems are found prevalent, then the better opinion is that such a country retains the characteristics of Dar-ul-Islam. From this it follows that Bulgaria, Greece, and other independent countries where Muslim Law is applied to the Muslims are Dar-ul-Islam. One of the tests whether a country is Dar-ul-Harb or Dar-ul-Islam is to ascertain whether congregational prayers on Fridays and Id (festival) days is held in that country or not, and on this ground India is held to be a Dar-ul-Islam, and further in India tne Muslim Law is applied in all matters of religion marrige, divorce, inheritance, gift and waqf, etc., to the Indian Muslims. The fact that the Muslim Criminal Law is not applied is not sufficient to change the character of Dar-ul-Islam.

Thus, we see that the relation determined by the Muslim Law between Muslims and non-Muslims has several aspects.

(1) Relation between the Muslim State and the non-Muslims living within its jurisdicrion.

(2) Relation between the non-Muslim State and the Muslims living within its jurisdiction.

(3) Relation between a Muslim State and a non-Muslim State.

The third is really the topic of International Law. According to the Shera the ruler of Dar-ul-Islam may lawfully declare Jihad against the non-Muslims of Dar-ul-Harb, but only for the protection of religion. Maulavi Cheragh Ali observes " the popular word Jihad occuring in several passages of the Koran, and generally construed by Christians and Moslems alike as meaning hostility or the waging of war against infidels, does not classically or literally signify war, warfare, hostility or fighting, and is never used in such a sense in the Koran".[1] The primary and original signification of the word Jihad is power ability and toil and its meaning as war is conventional and figurative. The change in the meaning of the word Jihad occured in the post-classical period long after the promulgation of the Holy Koran. In short, the Muslim Law maintains a clear distinction between the Dar-ul-Islam and Dar-ul-Harb, an act done in the Dar-ul-Harb may be devoid of legal consequences while the same act in the Dar-ul-Islam may be subject to legal restrictions. For instance there is no hadd or retaliation in the Dar-ul-Harb for the same act which is punishable in the Dar-ul-Islam.

---

1. A critical Exposition of the Popular Jihad, p. 163.

AL-ULUM-US-SHARIYAT.

The Muslim encyclopaedists have designated the appellation Al-ulum-us-shariyat to the science of Muslim religion and Jurisprudence.

According to our jurists "Al-ulum-us-shariyat" is divided into seven sections or four broad sub-divisions.[1]

I (1) Ilm-ul-Karat; the science of Reading the Koran.

(2) Ilm-at-Tafsîr, the science of the Interpretation of the Koran.

II (3) Ilm-al-Hadîs, the science of the Traditions.

(4) Ilm-ad-Dirâyat-al-Hadis, the science of critical discrimination in matters of Traditions.

III (5) Ilm-usul-addin, Ilm-al-Kalam, the science of Scholastic Theology.

IV (6) Ilm-usâl-al-Fiqh, the science of Principles of Jurisprudence.

(7) Ilm-ul-Fiqh, the science of Practical Jurisprudence.

I
The Koran.

The Koran may well be described as the final and the great legislative Code of Islam. It is the 'Fons publíc privatique iuris', 'Finis aequi iuris," and "Corpus Omnis *Muslim* iuris" of the science of Muslim Jurisprudence. The Koran is the divine communication and revelation to the Prophet of Islam. The Koran was in existence in manuscript form during the life time of the Prophet. It was also preserved in memory of the companions. Abu Bakr and Umar preserved this collection carefully. In A. H. 30 Usman finding some descripancies in the copies of the Koran which were circulated in the provinces, issued an official copy of the Koran, and all those copies in circulation were suppressed.

1. Von Hammer in Encyklopadische Uebersicht der Wissenschaften des Orients, p. 568 gives an admirable survey of the whole system. See also. W. H. Morley's Analytical Digest (The Muhammadan Law) p. CCXXVII.

The following are the eminent interpreters, writers of Tafsir of the Holy Koran.

(1) Abd Jafar Muhammad bin Jarir well known as the historian at-Tabari died (A. H. 310 A. D. 922)

(2) ‡ The Kashshaf by Abû-al-Qasim Jar ullah Mahmud bin Umar as-Zamakhshari died (A. H. 538 A. D. 1143)

(3) ‡ The Anwar-al-Tanzil by Nasir-uddin Abdallah bin Umr al-Baizâwî died (A. H. 685 A. D. 1286)

(4) The Yâkût-al-Táwíl, the Tafsir-al-Ghazali by Abû Hamîd Muhammad al-Ghazâlî (died A. H. 504 A. D. 110).

(5) The Durr-al-Mansur by Jalaluddin Abdur-Rahman bin Ali Bakr As-Suyûti died (A. H. 911 A. D. 1505).

(6) The Tafsir-al Jalalain by Jalaluddin Muhammad bin Ahmad Al-Mahalli (died A. H. 864 A. D. 1459) and by Jalal-uddin Abdul-Rahman bin Abu Bakr as-suyuti.

(7) Imam Fakhruddini-Razi. The Tafsir Kabir.

(8) The Tafsir Fath-al-Aziz by Shah Abdul-Aziz of Delhi.

(9) The Tafsirat Ahmadiyah by Mulla Jiwan Junpuri (during the reign of Aurangzib.)

The eminent Shia writers of Tafsir are :—

(1) Abu Jâfar Muhammad bin Babawiyat surnamed As-Saduk.

(2) Abu Jafar at-Turi The Mujmia-al Bayan li Ulum-al-Koran

(3) Nur-uddin Abdur-Rahman Jami.

(4) Kamal-uddin Husain al-Waiz-al-Kashefi, as Sabzawari. The Tafsir Husani.

II
The Hadis.

The Traditions consists of the actions precepts and teachings of the Prophet and their authenticity rests on the sunnat. They are classified into four divisions " Hadisul Matwatir Sahih, Hasan and Zaif," and the essential test is that they should not be contrary to the Koran. The first writers of Hadis, traditions, are :

(1) Abu Bakr bin Shihab Az Zuhri.

(2) Abdul-Malik bin Juraij.

(3) * Malik bin Anas (the Muwatta).

(4) * Muhammad Ibn Idris. Ash-Shafi'i (the Masnad and the Sunan).

(5) * Abu Abdillah Ahmad Ibn Hanbal. (The Masnadul Imam Hanbal).

‡ Both these works are universally respected by the Sunni Muslims
* The founders of the Maliki, Shafi'i and the Hanbali Sunn Schools of Jurisprudence.

The most eminent books of traditions are

(1) The Jamia-us-Sahih by Abu Abdullah Muhammad Ibn Ismaîîl al Bukhari (died A. H. 256 A. D. 869).[1]

(2) The Sahih Muslim by Abul-al-Husain Muslim bin Al-Hajaj bin Muslim of Nishapur (died A. H. 261 A. D. 874).

(3) The Jamia-wa-al-Ilal by Abu Isa Muhammad bin Isa at-Tirmizi (died A. H. 279 A. D. 892)

(4) The Kitab As-Sunan by Abu Dawud Sulaiman bin Al-Ashas surnamed As-Sajistani (died A. H. 275 A. D. 888.)

(5) Al-Mujtaba by Abu Abdur-Rahman Ahmad bin Ali bin Shuaib an Nasai.

(6) The Kitab as-Sunan by Abu Muhammad bin Yazid bin Majah al-Kazwini (died A. H. 273 A. D. 886.)

These six books are called Al-Kutub-as-Sittah fi-al-Hadis, and the first two of Bukhari and Muslim are by far the greatest authority. There are other collections also, important among them are.

(1) Abul Al-Husain Ali bih Umar ad-dariqutni (died A. H. 385 A. D. 995.)

(2) Abu Bakr Ahmad bin Al Husain al Baihaki (died A. H. 458 A. D. 1065.)

(3) Abu Muhammad Husain. bin Masud al Farra al Baghani.

(*i*) Jama bain al Sahihain.

(*ii*) The Masabih assunnat.

(4) Shaikh Waliudin Abu Abdullah Muhammad.

(*i*) Meshkat-al-Masabih.

The Shia jurists of the traditions are :—

(1) Abdullah bin Ali Al-Halabi.

(2) Abu Muhammad Hisham Ash Shaibani.

(3) Yunas bin Abdur-Rahman Al-Yuktaini.

(*i*) Ilal-al-Hadis.

(*ii*) Ikhtilaf al Hadis.

(4) Sheikh Abu Jafar at Tusi.

(*i*) Tahzib-al-Ahakam.

(*ii*) Istibsar.

(5) Muhammad bin Yakub Al-Kalini ar Razi.

(*i*) Kutub-i-Arbaa.

(6) Abu Jafar Muhammad Al-Kumi

(*i*) Man la Yazarhu al-Faqih.

(7) Abul-al-Abbas Ahmad bin Muhammad Ibn Ukdah.

(8) Ali bin Husain Al-Masudi.

(9) Abu-al-Faraj Ali bin Al-Husain al-Isfahani.

(10) Shaikh al-allamah Al-Hilli.

---

1. His compilation contains about 8000 traditions selected from a mass of 600,000 after a labour of 10 years.

The Juristic Development of the Muslim law.

III[1] and IV.

The Ilm al Fiqh is divided under two sections the Ilm-al-Fatawa which is known as the science of decisions and the Ilm-al-Faraiz the science the law of inheritance.

Ifta, Fatawas.

In connection with the Muslim administration of Justice, the Fatawas of the Jurists known as Mujtahids,[2] have played an important part. The opinions expressed by these doctors of law have virtually controlled the judiciary in administering justice. This is an anomaly which presents itself to a student of Muslim Jurisprudence. During the time of the Prophet only four persons, 'Umar 'Alî, Muâz and Abu Mûsâ were authorised to issue Fatawas and according to Imam Muhamma dthere were only six persons divided into two groups. They were authorised to issue Fatawas after joint consultation and deliberation. Alî, Ubayy and Abu Mûsâ were in one group. Umar, Zayd and Ibn Masud were in the other group.[3]

---

1. I don't propose to deal with the third head.

2. Imam Abu Yusuf said that giving a Fatwa is not permissible to any one but a Mujtahid.

A Mujtahid is defined in the Talwihthus: "A Muslim, wise, adult, intelligent by nature, well acquainted with the meaning of Arabic words and mandatory passages in the Koran, learned in the traditions of the Prophet, found in text books or orally reported, as as well as those which have have been abrogated."

تصحیح و فتح القدیز

1 ان ابا یوسف قال لایحل الفتوي الالمجتهد -

تلویح

و شرطه الاسلام والعقل والبلوغ ، کوله فقیه النفس اي شدید الفهم بالطبع و عالم باللغه العربیه و کونه حاویا بکتاب الله فیما یتعلق بالاحکام و عالما بالحدیث متنآ و سندآ و ناسخآ و منسوحا -

3 امام محمد کتاب الاثار - ستته من اصحاب النبی صلي الله علیه وسلم یتذکرون الفقه للوهم علي بن ابي طالب و ابي و ابو موسي ملحدة و عمر وزید و ابن مسعود ملحدة -

The first Khalifa Abu Bakr established the old Arabian precedent of deciding the issues by Ijma, the consensus of opinion of the first great followers of Islam. اکابر صحابه Umar followed this practice and the Fatawas passed by this deliberative body were circulated throughout the Muslim world. Shah Wali-ullah refers to this in the Hujjatullah-ul baligha.[1]

Umar also appointed such leading figures as Alî Usman Muâz bin Jabal, Abdur Rahman bin Awf, Ubayy bin Kab, Zayd bin Sabit and Abu Hurayra to issue Fatawas. Shah Wali-ullah definitely holds that it was not permissible to issue Fatwas without Khalifa's permission.[2]

This arrangement continued during the Khilafat of Usman and Ali who was himself a great jurist. However after the era of Khulafa-ur-rashidun the institution of *Ifta* declined, and no attempt was apparently made by the Umayyads or the Abbaside Kings to re-inaugurate, and establish it on permanent basis.[3] The Mujtahids however of their own accord continued to issue Fatawas on legal points submitted to them.

---

1 "It was the practice of Umar to consult and discuss the problems with the followers of the Prophet till the solution was free from doubt, and it is because of this that Fatawas given by Umar were acted upon throughout the East and West.

حجة الله البالغة

كان من سيرة عمر انه كان يشاور الصحابة ، ويناظرهم حتى تنكشف الغمة ، ويأتيه العلم فصار غالب قضاياه ، وفتاواه متبعة فى مشارق الارض ومغاربها .

2. Shâh Wali-ullah Izâlatul-khifâ:—

سابق وعظ و فتوی موقوف بود برائے خلیفه بود، امر خلیفه وعظ نمی گفتند و فتوی نمی دادند و اخر بغیر توقف برارائے خلیفه وعظ می گفتند و فتوی می دادند .

3. Of the later Muslim Kingdoms Turkey is the only country which established a special department called the Fatwa Khanah under the Grand Mufti who was given the appellation of Sheikh-ul-Islam by Muhammad II.

The multiplication of the fatawas without anybody to control its issue must have created a similar period as at Rome.[1]

Abdullah bin Masud had opened a School for the giving instructions in Fiqah. Some of his distinguished pupils like 'Alqamah and Aswad and their successors 'Ibrâhîm al Nakhaî had prepared a book containing the Fatawas [2] of the fourth Khalif Ali and those of Abdullah bin Masud. In 120 A. H. the great Imam Abu Hanifa was made the Head of this institution and he was the first to realise the necessity of establishing "a faculty of law," where legal problems could be debated and then published as authoritative opinion or combined Fatawas. The labours of this deliberative body were published in the form of a Code, Forty Jurists notably among then Kazi Abu Yûsuf, Daûd al-Tâiyy, Hafs Ibn Ghiyas Habban, Mandal, Yah a Ibn Abi Zâida, Qâsim bin Ma'n, Zufar and Imam Muhammad worked for a perid of thirty years to produce this gigantic Code. The publication of the Code was greeted with acclamations throughout the Muslim world. But unfortunately the Code was lost and we have no trace of it.

The authorship of Fiqh-i-Akbar is attributed by some to Abu Hanifa, while some well informed authorities doubt that to be his production. Of his works Masnadul Imam and a letter to Kazi Abu Yusuf have only come down to us. For his independent view and original thought Abu Hanifa had acquired the title of up-holder of private Judgment. The Fatawas of Imam Abu Hanifa had a binding affect on the decision of the Courts and it is related in Siratun-Nu'mân, that the famous Kazi Ibn Abî

---

1. At Rome some jurists were invested with the jus-respondendi (which is similar to the fatawas) and their works principally of Papinian, Paulus Gaius, Ulpian and Modestins had acquired a prescriptive authority. The multiplication of the Responsas created difficulties and the remedy provided by the law of Citations enacted by Theodosius II and Valentinian III in A. D. 426 was "that the opinion of the majority should prevail and if the numbers were equal the view of Papinian should be applied."

2. Shiblî Sîratun-Numân (in Urdu), p. 193.

Layla who had served on the bench for 33 years, was once much annoyed by Imam Abu Hanifa's creticisms on his judgments that he reported to the Governor of Kufa, that the great Imam should be stopped from issuing Fatawas. The Governor reluctantly issued the order with which the Imam complied. This inicdent once more illustrate that jurists can only issue Fatawas with direct permission (at least by tacit consent) of the ruling power.

The present Hanafi jurisprudence consists mainly of the commentaries written by various authors on the works and opinions of Imam Abu Hanifa. In some cases the opinions of the great Imam have been superseded with the consent of all the jurists and the view of one or more of the disciples has been accepted *in toto*. But there is no such general rule that in case of conflict between the great Imam and his two chief disciples the view of Májority should be adopted.[1]

"The age of Abu Hanifa was the age of jurists." At Medina Imam Malik had established the Maliki School and his pupil Imam Shafi'î founded the Shafi'î School. Imam Shafi 'i's pupil, Imam Hanbal, founded the fourth and the last of the Sunni Schools of jurisprudence.

These four great Imams were recognised as Mujtahids by the Muslims. There is not much difference in the fundamental Islamic principles enunciated by these four Schools, they only differ in minor details [2]. These Sunni Schools are

1. The opinion expressed by Mahmood, J. in Abdul Kadir v. Salima, 8 All., 149, is incorrect. Mahmood, J. observed that "it is a general rule of interpretation of the Muhammadan Law that in cases of difference of opinion among the jurisconsults Imam Abu Hanifa and his two disciples Quazi Abu Yusuf and Imam Muhammad the opinion of the Majority must be followed and in the application of legal principles to temporal matters the opinion of Quazi Abu Yusuf is entitled to the greatest weight." See criticisim in the Muslim Law of marriage by the present author, p. xxxix.

2. The development of Law by these four Schools may favourably compare with the rise of the Humanists the French historical School in the 16th century, or to that of Hugo and Savigny's School of jurisprudence.

admittedly indebted to the juristic School of Medina headed, by the great Imam Baqr, and his son Jâfâr as Sadiq. Imam Abu Hanifa himself had attended the School of Medina.

The eminent jurist of the Sunni Hanafi School of Jurisprudence are :—

Before the time of Imam Abu Hanifa.
Abdullah Ibn Masud.
Abdullah Ibn Abbas.
Utaba ibn Masud.
Alqamah.
Aswad.
Ibrahim Nakha'i.

Imam Abu Hanifa's contemporaries and whose lectures he attended were numerous, their number is over sixty-five. Some of them are :—

Imam Baqr.
Imam Jafar as Sadiq.
Hammadbin Abi Sulaiman.
Qatadah.
Al'Amash.
Nafa'y Maula ibn Umar.
Musa bin Abi Aaysha.
Ibn Shab Zahry.
Akramah Maula ibn Abbas.
Abdullah bin Dinar.
Abdurrahman bin Harmuz.
Ibrahim bin Muhammad.
Jabala Ibn Sahim.
Qasim Masudi.
'Aun bin Abdullah.
Ali bin Aqmar.
Ata bin Abi Rabah.
Said bin Musruk Suri.
Salmah bin Khel.
Samak bin Harab.
Amir Sabey.
Ata bin Saib.
Mahammad bin Saib.
Maharib bin Dasar.
Hasham bin Urwah.
Yahya bin Said.
'Abu ulzbyrmaki.

*The Hanafi School.**

Imam Abu Hanifa the jurisconsults and founder of the Hanafi School.

The Great Imam's well-known pupils are:—
Kazi Abu Yusuf.
Muhammad bin Hasan.
Daud at-Taiyy.
Hasan ibn Ziad.

---

*"Learned men well versed in the Fiqha have held that the field of Fiqha was cultivated (zar) by Abdullah bin Masud was irrigated (saqqa) by Alqamah, was reaped (hasad) by Ibrahim-un-Nakhi was thrased (dassa) by Hammad who separated the corn from the chaff, was ground and pounded (tahan) by Abu Hanifa. was kneaded (ajan) by Abu Yusuf, was converted into bread (khabiz) by Muhammad bin Hasan and the rest of the world are mere eaters thereof."

Abdul-Razak bin Hamám.

Yahya Ibn Abi Zaida Kazi of Madayn.

Yazid bin Hasan.

Hafs ibn Ghiyas, Kazi of Baghdad.

Abul Asam ulnabiel.

Habban.

Mandal.

Qasim ibn Má'n, Kazi of Kufa.

Yusuf bin Khalid.

Asad bin Umra, Kazi of Baghdad.

Afia bin Yazid.

Ali bin Almushar, Kazi of Musul.

Yahya bin Saed-ul-Qatan.

Abdullah bin Almubarak.

Vakie bin ul Jarah.

Abu Muty Balkhi.

Hamad bin Abu Hanifa.

The following are the well-known books on the Muslim Jurisprudence.[1]

The Adab-al-Kazi by Imam Abu Yusuf.

The Adab-al-Kazi by Abu Bakr Ahmad al-Khassaf.

The Al-Fiqh-al-Akbar (by Imam Shafi.)

The Al-Usul by Fakhrul Islam Abul Hasan Ali Bazdawi.

* The Al-ayatul Bayinanet by Ahmad ibn Qasim.

The Al Mohit by Abu Bakr Muhammad as-Sarakhsi.

The Ashbah-wa-Nazair by Zain-ul-Aabidin Almisri.

‡ The Alshara-ul-Kabir by Sheikh Muhammad bin Ahmad.

§ Alfrat-ul-Faiz by Sheikh Ali Qasim.

The Badaia al-Mubtada by Burhanuddin Ali-al-Marghiani.

The Bahr-ar-Raiq by Zainul-Abidin al-Misri and Seraj-uddin Umar.

The Bighyat-ul-Bahis by Abi Abdullah ibn al-Mutakawwah.

§ Bidaya-ul-Mujtahad wa Nihayat-ul-Muqtised by Alwalid Muhammad.

The Durar-al-Hukkam by Mulla Khusru.

The Durrul-Mukhtar by Alauddin Muhammad.

The Fawaid by Hamiduddin Al Bukhari

The Fathul-Qadir by Kamal-uddin Muhammad as-Siwasi.

The Fatwa Alamgiri by the order of Emperor Aurangzib.

The Fatawa Ahu by Maj-uddin Asad.

The Fatawa Kazi Khan by Imam Fakhruddin Hasan Kazi Khan

The Fatawa-an-Nawawi by An Nawawi

The Fatawa Ahl Samakand.

---

1. See the Bibiographical doctionaries, the Khasf-az-Zunun, of Haji Khalifah, of Ibn Khalkan, of an-Nawawi, the Tabakat-al-Fukha of Abu Ishaq Ash-shirazi and see also Maulana Sheikh Abdul awal Jaunpuri Mufid-ul-Mufti (in Urdu) recently published in A. H. 1326.

The Fatawa Ibrahim Shahi (of Jaunpore.)

The Fatawa Anqirvi by Muhammad bin al Husain al-Auqirvi.

The Fatawa Hammadiyah by Abulal-Fath Rukunuddin.

The Fatawa-i-Muhammadi by the order of Tipu Sultan.

The Fatawa-i-Sirajiyah by Sirajuddin.

The Fatawa-i-Buzaziyah by Sheikh Hafizuddin Ibn al bazaz.

The Fatawa-Ibn Firkah by Ibn Firkah.

The Fatawa Ibn as-Salah by Abu Amru Usman Ash Shahrazuri.

The Fatawa-az-Zainuyat by Zainul Abidin Ibrahim al-Misri.

The Fatawa az Zahiriga by Zahiruddin Abu Bakr Muhammad

The Fatawa-i-Nakshbandiyah. by Khawaja Mu'inuddin.

The Fatawa-i-Kasakhani by Mulla Sudruddin.
al-Bukhari.

The Fatawa Tatarkhaniyah by Imam Aalim bin Ala-al Hanafi.

The Fatawa-i-Abdur Rahman by Mufti Abdur Rahman of Turkey.

The Faraiz al-Fazari by Ibn Firkah.

The Fiqh al Akbar (authorship is attributed to Imam Abu Hanifa.)

The Fuṣul-al Isturushi by Muhammad al-Isturushi.

The Fusul al-Imadiyat by Abul al-Fath as-Samarkandi.

The Ghayat ul Bayan by Imamuddin Amir.

† The Ghayat-ul Ahkam by Jamaluddin Hasan bin Yusuf.

The Ghurar-ul Ahkam by Mulla Khusru.

The Hamavi by Ahmad bin Muhammad.

The Hedaya by Burhanuddin Ali Abu Bakr al-Marghiani.

‡ Hidayat-ul-Talibin by Muhammad Amir.

‡ Hidayat-ul-Mutabid by Sheikh Salih.

The Inayah by Akmaluddin Muhammad bin Mahmud.

The Jamià-ul Kabir by Imam Muhammad.

The Jamia us-Sagbir by Imam Muhammad.

† The Jamia ash Shraia by Yahya ibn Ahmad al-Helli.

† The Jamia-i-Abbasi by Muhammad Aamili.

† The Jamia ush-Shittat.

The Jami-ur Rumuz by Shamsuddin Muhammad al-Khurasani.

* The Jam-ul-Jawami by Tajuddin Subki.

The Jawahra-ul-Kalam.

The Kafi Abdullah bin Ahmad Hefizuddin An-Nasafi.

The Kifayah by Imamuddin Amir.

The Kashf, by Abu Jafar.

The Kanz-ul-Absar by Shamusuddin Muhammad.

The Kanz-ud-dakaik by Hafizuddin An-Nasafi.

* The Kitab-al-Wasait by Abu Ibrahim Ismail Al-Muzaini.

The Kitab-fi-al Fiqhal Qudusi by Hafiz Muhammad Al-Qudusi.

The Kurat-ul-Ayoon by Ibnu Abidin.

The Kitabul Khiraj by Imam Abu Yusuf.

The Khulasat al-akuwl by Jamaluddin Hasan bin Yusuf.

The Khulasat al-Fatawa by Imam Iftikaruddin al-Bukhari.

The Kunyat al-Munyat by Mukhtar bin Mahmud Najmuddin.

The Khizanatul Fatawa by Ahmad bin Muhammad.

† The Lamah-i-Dimiskiya by Abdullah Ash-Shami.

The Mabsut-fi-furua al-Hanafiyat by Imam Muhammad.

The Mabsut (in II Vols.) by Fakhrul Islam Bazdawi.

The Mabsut by Abu Bakr al-Sarakhsi.

The Majmu-ul-Nawazil by Ahmad bin Isa.

The Matlab-al-Faik by Badruddin Muhammad ad Dairi.

* The Mansur / The Mukhtasar } by Abu Ibrahim al Muzaini.

* * The Minhajet Tablin by Mohiuddin Abu Zakaria an-Nawawi.

The Munhal-ul-Khaliq by Ibnu Abidin.

The Mukhtasar by Ibn Hajib.

The Muktasar (commentary) by Kazi Udud.

† The Mukhtaiaf Ashshia by Jamaluddin Hasan bin Yusuf.

† The Mufateh by Muhammad bin Murtaza Muhsan.

† The Mukhtusar-i-Nafia by an unknown Writer.

† The Mujanad-fi al Fikh wa Alfatawa by Abu Jafar-at-Tusi.

The Multaka al Abhar by Ibrahim al-Halabi.

The Majmai-ul Anhar by Shaikh zada Abdur Rahman.

The Majmaiul Bahrin by Muzafaruddin Ahmad.

The Mukhtsar-at-Tahavi by Abu Jafar Ahmad bin Muhammad at-Tahavi.

The Mukhtasar al-Qudri by Abu al-Husain Ahmad al-Qudri.

‡ Muwahib aljalil by Abdullah Muhammad.

‡ Mukhtasar-ul Alama by Sheikh Khalil.

The Nahr-ul-Faikh by Zainulabidin Almisri and Sirajuddin Umar.

The Nawadir by Imam Muhammad.

The Nikayah by Husmuddin Husain bin Ali.

The Nikayah (Makhtasar al-Wikayah) by Ubaidullah bin Masud.

* The Nihayat el Muhtaj by Shamusuddin Muhammad.

The Raddul Muhtar by Muhammad Amin Ibnu Abidin.

The Ramz-al-Haqaiq by Badruddin Mahmud al Aaini.

* The Rasail ul Muatabisa by Abu Ibrahim al-Muzani.

The Sharifiyah by Sayyid Sharif Ali bin Muhammad al-Jurjani.

The Sharh-ul-Wikayah by Ubaidullah bin Masud.

† The Sharaia-ul-Islam by Majmuddin Abul al-Kasim Jafar al Hilli.

† The Shara-i-looma by an unknown author.

‡ Shara Ulalama by Ahmad bin Muhammad.

The Sirajiyah by Sirajuddin Muhammad as-Sajamandi.

The Siyar-al-Kabir wa as-Saghir by Imam Muhammad.

The Siraj-ul-Wahaj by Abu Bakr bin Ali.

‡ Tabasarat-ul Ahkam wa Minhaj-ul Ahkam by Burhanudddin Ibrahim.

The Tabyin-al-Haqaiq by Fakhruddin Abu Muhammad Az-zailani.

The Talwih by Saduddin Taftazani.

The Tauzih by Sadrush-Shariat.

The Tahtavi by Sayyid Ahmad Tahtavi.

*The Tuhfat el Muhtaj.

† The Tahrir-al-Ahkam by Jamaluddin Hasan bin Yusuf

The Tanwirul-Absar by Shamsuddin Muhammad al-Ghazzi.

The Taqrir wa Tahbir by Ibn Hamman.

The Tatarkhania by Alim bin Alai.

The Tuhfat al-Fukaha by Ala-uddin Muhammad Assawarqandi.

The Tuhfat as-Sukuk by Nuaman Effendi.

The Umdal-ul-Riayah by Maulana Abdul Hai.

The Wafi by Hafizuddin An-Nasafi.

The Wikayah by Burhan Ash Shariyat Mahmud.

The Zakhiratul-Fatawa by Burhanuddin Bukhari.

The Zahir ar-Rawayat (The Reports of Imam Muhammad).

The Ziyadat fi furua al-Hanafiyat by Imam Muhammad.

Dr. Snouck Hurgronje and some of the Dutch and German thinkers were so impressed by the the jurisprudential side of the Islamic Shera that they came to the conclusion that it never had an "important practical side. Similarly Dr. Goldziher observes: "In later days, historical consideration has proved that only a small part of this system, connected with religious and family life, has a practical

*—Denotes books of the Shafii School of Jurisprudence.

†—Denotes books of the Shia School of Jurisprudence.

‡ Denotes books of the Maliki School of Jurisprudence.

§ Denotes books of the Haubali School of Jurisprudence.

The rest of the books are on the Hanafi Jurisprudence.

effect as of old, while in many parts of merely juristical character this theological law is entirely put aside in actual jurisdiction............Snouck Hurgronje was really the first who set forth with great acuteness and sure judgment the historical truth, namely, that what we call Muhammedan law is nothing but an *ideal* law, a theoretical system, in a word, a learned school-law, which reflects the thoughts of pious theologians about the arrangement of Islamic society, whose sphere of influence was, willingly extended by pious rulers—as far as possible—but which as a whole could hardly ever have been the real practical standard of public life.............Even the penalties for offences against religious laws are often nothing, else but ideal claims of the pious, dead letters conceived in studies and fostered in the hearts of God-fearings scholars, but neglected and suppressed in life where other rules become prevailing..."[1]

The above observations of an eminent scholar of the Muslim polity are to some extent correct, it is true that the old Shera of Islam has suffered a progressive modification upon the area of its practical application, but surely Dr. Hurgronje and Goldziher would not like us to execute in the present century the rigid punishments prescribed by the Muslim penal law, and does not the very verses of the Koran suggests to us better alternatives? Why not adopt these alternatives. If the Muslim Shera because of its development by the jurists is stigmatised as the ideal law with no practical side, then likewise all developed systems of jurisprudence whether the Roman, or English or German, should also be designated as ideal codes. The truth is that the fundamental principles of the Shera are the foundation on which the vast amount of Muslim jurisprudence is based, and is developed in harmony with the requirements and customary laws of every Muslim country. The Muslim law of to-day is nothing more

1. Snouck Hurgronje in Revue de l' Histoire des Religions, XXVII Goldziher in Zeitschrift fur Vergleichende Rechtswissenschaft, VIII, p. 406. A. H. Lybyer the Ottoman Empire in the time of Suleiman, p. 154.

than the Muslim—Arabian law, the Muslim—Turkish law, the Muslim—Egyptian law, the Muslim—Persian law and the Muslim—Indian law.

Development of Law.

Law is developed by a process of interpretation and by private judgment. The guiding factor is to secure the ends of justice. While it is true that the Koranic law of Islam is unalterable and unchangeable, however a wide latitude is given by Shera for the expansion of law. We have seen from the tradition reported by Muaz bin Jabal that the Prophet of Islam had approved of deciding cases when the Koran and the traditions were silent on the point in accordance with private Judgment. This is technically known as Ijtihad, its scope was very wide. The Fatawa Alamgiri says accordingly, "When there is neither written law, nor concurrence of opinions, for the guidance of a Kazi, if he be capable of legal disquisition and have found a decisive judgment on the case, he should carry such judgment into effect by his sentence, although other scientific lawyers may differ in opinion from him, for that which, upon deliberate investigation, appears to be right and just, is accepted as such in the sight of God."

According to Sir Henry Maine the chief agencies by which the progress of law is affected are in their historical order Legal Fictions, Equity and Legislation. Fiction is "any assumption which conceals, or affects to conceal, the fact that a rule of law has undergone alteration its letter remaining unchanged, its operation being modified."[1] In the Roman law the Fiction of Adoption, the interpretation of the pontifices and that of the prudentes are notable examples. Similarly under the Muslim law the doctrine of Ijtihad, and later juristic deduction technically known as analogy, Qiyas," are instances of development of law by legal Fictions The function of analogy is to extend the law of the text, the theory being that the newly discovered law though

1. Maine's Ancient Law, p. 29.

not covered by the lauguage of the text is governed by the reason of the text. Mr. Abdur Rahim points out that "the writers on jurisprudence do not admit that extension of law by process of analogy amounts to establishing a new rule of law."[1]

The next stage is the development of law by Equity. "The Equity whether of the Roman Praetors or of the English Chancellors, differs from the Fictions which in each case preceded it, in that the interference with law is open and avowed."[2] It seems to possess a superior sanctity. The introduction of Jus Naturale illustrate the influence of Praetorian equity in the Roman law and the point of contact between the Jus Gentium, and Jus Naturale was this notion of "Aequitas," a levelling influence. In the Muslim law Imam Abu Hanifa supplemented this process of law and called it Istehsan. Thus a jurist was permitted to devise a rule of law in the interest of justice and public welfare. The Hanafi jurists speak of Istehsan as hidden analogy; the other three Schools opposed this innovation, and Imam Shafi'i retorted "whoever resorts to Istehsan makes law.' But in course of time they were forced to modify their views, and Imam Malik, founded the doctrine of public good "Muslahat", a process similar to juristic equity, and followed it up by inventing Istidlal a distinct method of juristic ratiocination which the Shafi'i also accepted. Kazi Udud says, that the Hanafi doctrines of Istehsan, and the Maliki doctrine of public good are covered up by Istidlal. The development of law by Istehsan, Muslahat and Istidlal is the period of juristic Equity in the Muslim law.

Legislation is the last agency to com e into operation, as a suitable and proper means of effecting alterations in the laws governing civilised communities. It differs from Legal Fictions and just as much from Equity as "Its obligatory

1. Muhammadan Jurisprudence, p. 139.
2. Maine's Ancient Law, p. 33.

force is independent of its principles." In the Muslim countries the edicts of the Kings for instance the kanun-nameh of the Sultans of Turkey are good examples of direct legislation on points not covered by the Shera. The doctrine of Ijma which is defined as the consensus of opinion among the jurists in a particular age on a question of law, is a notable example of legislation by the jurists in Muhammadan law. The codification of Roman law under Justinian, and partial codification and enactments relating to the Muslim law, notably the modern Egyptian code of Hanafi law of Muhammad Kadri Pasha and various enactments in Turkey and other countries, and in India for instance the Waqf Acts of 1913 and 1923 are the latest agencies in the development of the Shera of Islam.

But the Muslim law was greatly developed in a movement parallel to the Responsa Prudentium of Roman law. Bryce has correctly remarked " In the East, as for instance, in such countries as Turkey or Persia, there is little that can be called general legislation. Hatts are no doubt occasionally promulgated by the Sultan, though they are sometimes not meant to be observed, and are frequently not in fact observed. So far as new law is made, it is made by the learned men who study and interpret the Koran and the vast mass of tradition which has grown up round the Koran. The existing body of Musulman law has been built up by these doctors of law during the last twelve centuries, but chiefly in the eighth and ninth centuries of our era ; and a vast body it is."[1] "No system of law is the product of a single mind or age,"[2] the divine communications of the Holy Koran laid down only the fundamental principles, and the entire bulk of the Muslim jurisprudence is the result of development and expansion, by juristic interpretation and

1. Studies in History and Jurisprudence, Vol. II, p. 253.

2. "Law is the product of the entire history of a people, an evolution, by organic growth." Dr. Sherman, Roman law in the modern world, p. 232.

judicial dicta, by legislation and codification, covering centuries of constant labour on the study of the "Shera" itself, and the comparative jurisprudence of other legal systems of the world. "We all recognise now that law has grown by conscious efforts towards the solution of social problems conditioned by causes which spring from previous stages of development and from the influence of surroundings.... Evolution in this domain means a constant struggle between two conflicting tendencies the certainty and stability of legal systems and progress and adaptation to circumstances in the order to achieve social justice."[1]

1. Vinogradoff, P. "Historical Jurisprudence," Vol. I, p. 146.

—:o:—

BIBLIOGRAPHY.*

Abdul Awal; Mufid-ul-Mufti (Urdu).

Abdur Rahim; Muhammadan Jurisprudence.

Aitchison C.; A collection of Treaties, India.

Al-Badaoin (tr. by G. S. A Ranking); Muntakhabu Tawarikh (3 Vols.).

Ameer Ali; A short History of the Saracens.

Ameer Ali; Mahomedan Law (2 Vols).

Anson. W. R.; Law and custom of the Constitution. (2 Vols).

Archbold, W. A. J.; Indian Constitutional history.

Aristotle; The Politics.

Arnold T. W.; The Caliphate.

Austin J.; Jurisprudence.

Banerjea P.; Public Administration, in Ancient India.

Bentham J.; Braught for the organisation of Judicial establishments.

Beni Prasad; History of Jahangir.

Bernier; The Travels.

Beveridge A. S.; The Emperor Akbar.

Blackstone W.; Commentaries on the Laws of England.

Bluntschli, J. K.; The Theory of the State.

Blochmann H.; The Ain-i-Akbari,

Bodin J.; De Republica.

* The Books on the Muslim Jurisprudence are stated on pp. 115,116 and 121—125.

The Imperial enactments and acts of the Government of India and Regulations of the East India Company and Law Reports are noted in their proper places.

Browne E G.; A literary History of Persia.

Bryce J.; Studies in History and Jurisprudence.

Bryce J.; American Commonwealth (Vol. 1)

Buhler G.; The Laws of Manu.

Cicero M. T. de; Republica.

Cheragh Ali; Criticial exposition of the Jihad.

Cowell H. Courts and Legislative Authorities.

Creasy E.; The History of the Ottoman Turks.

Cromer Earl of; Modern Egypt (2 Vols).

Das A. C.; Rgvedic Culture.

Davey R.; The Sultan and his Subjects (2 Vols).

Dicey A. V.; Law of the Constitution.

Dozy R.; The Spanish Islam.

D'Ohsson C. M.; Tableau general de'Empire Othoman.

Duguit; Traite de droit Constitutionnel.

Elliot H. M.; The History of India (8 Vols).

Fathul Baldan.

Fifth Report of the Select Committee of the House of Commons.

Finch W.; Purchas IV.

Ganganatha Jha; Studies in Hindu Law.

Goldziher I.; Zeitschrift fer Vergleichende Rechtswissenschaft.

Grady G.; the Hedaya (Hamilton).

Greene E. B.; The Foundations of American Nationality.

Habibur Rahman Khan; Sirat-as-Siddiq (Urdu).

Hamilton C.; The Hedaya.

Hammer J. Von; Des Osmanischen Reichs staatsverfassung.

Hammer J. Von; Encyklopadische Ubersicht dar Wissenschaften des Orients.

Heidborn A.; Manuel de droit public et administratif de l'empire Ottoman.

Hobbes T. The works of Leviathan.

Imam Muhammad; Kitab-alasar.

Ishwri Prasad; Medieval India.

Jarrett H. S.; History of the Caliphs by Jalaluddin as Sayuti.

Jarett H. S.; Ain-i-Akbari.

Jayaswal K. P.; Hindu Polity.

Jellinek; AllgemeineStaatslehre.

Jung, ibn S. Md. Ullah; The Muslim Law of Marriage.

Kadri Pasha; The Egyptian Hanafi Code.

Khuda Bukhsh; S. Contributions to the History of Islamic Civilization.

Khuda Bukhsh; S. The Orient under the Caliphs.

Khalilur-Rahman. M. tr. of Nafhut-Tib of Al-Maqqari (Urdu).

Krabbe H.; The modern idea of the state. tr. by G. H. Sabine and W. J. Shepard. 1

Kremer A. Von: Culturgeschichte des Orients.

Kremer A. Von; Culturgeschichtliche Streifzuge Auf Dem Gebiete Des Islams.

Laband; Staatsrecht des deutschen Reicht.

Lanepoole S.; Mediæval India.

Larpent J.; Turkey, its History and Progress.

Leyden J. and Erskine W.; Memoirs of Babar.

Lybyer A. H.; The Ottoman Empire in the time of Suleiman.

Lybyer A. H.; The Turkish Parliament Proceedings of the American Political Science Association, Vol. VII.

Macdonald D. B.; The Development of Muslim theology.

Maine H. S.; Early Law and Custom.

Maine H. S.; Ancient Law.

Malcolm J.; The History of Persia (2 Vols).

Manucci N.; Storia (4 Vols).

Mazhr-ul-Haq; Sawanih Umri Umar II (Urdu).

Mirat-i-Ahmadi.

Montesquieu; De lesprit des lois.

Morison T.; Imperial rule in India.

Muir W.; The life of Mahomet.

Muir W.; The Caliphate.

Morley W. H.; An Analytical Digest.

Muhammad Khan S.; The History of Spain (Urdu).

Muhammad Ali; The Quran.

Narada (Jolly); Legal Procedure.

Nicholson R.; A literary history of the Arabs.

O'leary de Lacy; History of the Fatimid Khalifate.

Ovington; Voyage to Sura[illegible]

Plato Republic.

The Pioneer, Nov. 4th an[illegible] De[illegible] 14th 1925.

The Pioneer Feb. 21 and March 5th, 1926.

Qanungo K., Sher Shah.

Rogers and Beveridge: Memoirs of Jahangir.

Sarbuland Jung Bahadur Nawab, Leaves from the Diary to an Attache to the Earl of Northbrook.

Sarkar J. N.: The Mughal Administration.

Sarkar J. N.; The History of Aurangzib (5 Vols.)

Seydel Von.; Bayerisches Staatsrecht.

Shah Khan Md.: Hayat Siddiq Akbar (Urdu).

Sherman C. P.; Roman Law in the Modern World

Shibli; Alfaruq. (Urdu).

Shibli: Risail. (Urdu).

Shibli: Siratun-Naman (Urdu).

Shibli: Siratun-Nabi (Urdu).

Snouck Hurgronje, le droit Musulman; Revue de l' Histoire des Religious, XXXVII.

Stoddard L.; The New World of Islam.

Thompson W. F.; tr. of the Akhalk-i-Jalalry.

Thevenot Monsieur de.; The Travels.

Ubicini A.; Letters Surerla Turquie.

Van Ben Berg L. W. C. and E. C. Howard; tr of Minhaj et Talibin.

Vambery H. A.; Western Culture in Eastern Lands.

Virogradoff P.; Historical Jurisprudence (2 Vols.)

Wilson R. K.; Digest of Anglo-Muhammadan Law.

Wilson Woodrow; The State.

Waliullah Shah Hujjat-ulbaligha

Waliullah Shah; Izalatul Khifa an Khilafatil Khulafa

Zulkader Jung Bahadur Nawab: Khilafat-i-Andalusia (Urdu).

Abbreviation.

All.=The Indian Law Repor[ts] Allahabad Series

Cal.=The Indian Law Reports Calcutta Series

Jud. Reg.=Judicial Regulation.

Beng.=Bengal.